ON BEING QUEER, BLACK, BRILLIANT . . . AND COMPLETELY OVER IT

LESTER FABIAN BRATHWAITE

Tiny Reparations Books

An imprint of Penguin Random House LLC
penguinrandomhouse.com

LIBRARY OF CONGRESS CATALOGING-IN-PUBLICATION DATA

Names: Fabian Brathwaite, Lester, author.
Title: Rage: on being queer, black, brilliant . . . and completely over it / Lester Fabian Brathwaite.
Description: New York: Tiny Reparations Books, 2024.
Identifiers: LCCN 2024000484 (print) | LCCN 2024000485 (ebook) | ISBN 9780593185087 (hardcover) | ISBN 9780593185094 (epub)
Subjects: LCSH: Fabian Brathwaite, Lester, author. | Periodical editors—United States—Biography. | African American authors—Biography. | Gay authors—United States—Biography.
Classification: LCC PN4874.F386575 A3 2024 (print) | LCC PN4874.F386575 (ebook) | DDC 070.92 [B]—dc23/eng/20240207
LC record available at https://lccn.loc.gov/2024000484
LC ebook record available at https://lccn.loc.gov/2024000485

Printed in the United States of America

1st Printing

BOOK DESIGN BY ALISON CNOCKAERT

For my mom . . .

though, were she here, I'd definitely urge
her *not* to read this book.

CONTENTS

1

FUCKING WHITE BOYS • 1

2

I WORSHIP AT THE ALTAR OF HIS BODY • 27

3

NIGGER LOVER • 53

4

MEMOIR OF A BLOUSE • 79

5

THE IMPOSSIBILITY OF LOVE • 105

6

I HATE THE GAYS • 133

7

VICTIM OR VILLAIN? • 159

8

GIFTED • 187

9

SILENCE • 215

10

RAGE • 241

ACKNOWLEDGMENTS • 267

NOTES • 269

1

FUCKING WHITE BOYS

ONE OF THE first, if not *the* first, published bits of Black, gay prose—and for all intents and purposes and for the remainder of this book, when I say "gay," I mean almost exclusively "gay cisgender male"—was Richard Bruce Nugent's "Smoke, Lilies and Jade."

One passage opens with the main character, Alex, searching in a field "on his hands and knees," until he finds at last "two strong white legs . . . dancer's legs . . . the contours pleased him . . . his eyes wandered . . . on past the muscular hocks to the firm white thighs . . . the rounded buttocks . . . then the lithe narrow waist . . . strong torso and broad deep chest . . . the heavy shoulders . . . the graceful muscled neck . . . squared chin and quizzical lips . . . Grecian nose with its temperamental nostrils . . . the brown eyes looking at him . . . like . . . Monty looked at Zora . . . his hair curly and black and all tousled . . . and it was Beauty . . ."

This short story was published in 1926 in the first and only issue of the nevertheless highly influential *Fire!!* magazine, which was founded and filled by some of the greats of the Harlem Renaissance. Alongside poetry, plays, essays, and short stories by Langston Hughes, Countee Cullen, Zora Neale Hurston, and Wallace Thurman sat Nugent's gay-ass prose. Openly gay. Openly ass.

A lot of the Harlem Renaissance luminaries were queer in some way, but it was an aspect of their lives that was often obfuscated in their work and in their later biographies. Subtitled "A Novel, Part 1," "Smoke, Lilies and Jade" is, as a work of literature, *a'ight*. Nugent wrote it when he was twenty, and it reads like something I might have written in college. While some writers do amazing work at that age, I was not one of them, and neither was Nugent. No tea; no shade; no smoke, lilies, or jade.

The story is all very stream of consciousness with no proper sentences, just clauses separated by ellipses, the kind of novelistic experimentation that seemed to be all the rage back then— with the previous year's *Mrs. Dalloway* among the best examples—but Nugent didn't have the range to pull it off, not yet anyway. Still, Nugent does have a poetic lilt to his words that's appealing, and one wonders what the rest of this novel could have been had he finished it. And it's a good story—it would've gotten an A in college, and it made the single issue of *Fire!!*, where it fits in perfectly as part of that magazine's manifesto to give voice to the young, radical Black creatives shaking the tree of American culture out of a few square blocks in New

York. Therefore, as a work of transgressive art, "Smoke, Lilies and Jade" is fucking astounding.

The story's protagonist, Alex, a clear stand-in for Nugent, is a struggling artist, living with his mother and chronically unemployed, though he also happens to be close consorts with people named Zora, Countee, and Langston. Alex is bisexual—*but is she, though?* He's ostensibly in a relationship with some poor girl named Melva, but he's completely obsessed with this white boy Adrian, whom he calls Beauty. He claims to be in love with Melva, who, it seems, is also white, but he fixates on Beauty. An entire passage is dedicated to Alex and Beauty lying in bed together, the sleeping Beauty's hair tickling Alex's nose as he smokes beside him, all the while wanting to kiss his beautiful lips.

Again, this is something I might have written in college, or in those wandering years after I had dropped out, when my desire gnawed at my insides and the only reprieve was the fictions I constructed around beautiful white boys. Once I finally started getting it in, as the kids say, I was able to turn the fictions into reality and wrote those moments as memories in my head. I came to understand why so many gay writers delight in describing the nape of a man's neck; the softness of their hair and the way it decorates a pillow; the soft, soft eyelashes veiling secret treasures of the world; the parted lips aching to be kissed; the skin always white, always white, always white.

So much of gay literature fixates on white male beauty (and its destruction)—from Oscar Wilde's *The Picture of Dorian Gray* to James Baldwin's *Giovanni's Room* to the seminal gay novels of 1978 to Alan Hollinghurst's *The Sparsholt Affair.* So much of anything intended for a gay audience fixates on and exalts white male beauty. Is it any wonder, then, that I have always fixated on and exalted white male beauty, when the things I sought to teach me how to *be* all taught the same thing: that white boys are beauty, white boys are desire? It all comes down to fucking white boys.

I CAME TO America in 1990 from Guyana, a tiny island-nation off the coast of Africa. Just kidding, it's a mostly landlocked country in South America, but I had you going there for a minute. America blew my stupid four-year-old mind: Cable television? Are you *fucking kidding me?* Malls! Food that was fast and, I assumed, good for you—otherwise, why would they make it so cheap and readily available? It's not like Guyana was "the third world" when that was still a legitimate way to describe countries—after all, noted white American man Jim Jones seemed to like it enough . . . too much, some might say— but it certainly wasn't the first world. I don't have any memories of it, really, but we didn't have HBO. America was so rich and white and big and loud compared to the mostly Black and brown, very poor, pretty small land of my birth. I hadn't quite figured out what being gay was, but I did have a tacit understanding that whatever it was, to quote the great Valerie Cherish, "I'm it!" And I should probably keep quiet about it.

But I fell in love so easily with men. Men in magazines, on television, in film. They weren't all necessarily white men, but being that most of the men anywhere were white, they tended

4

to be. My first loves were *Saved by the Bell*'s Zack Morris and *Blossom*'s Joey Russo. My mother loved her daytime soap operas, and so did I, because soaps had a reliable stream of shirtless hunks who were always *just* coming out of the shower or *just* about to put on a shirt or *just* lying around suggestively naked after making softly lit love to a woman. And then I started to fall in love with men in real life.

In school, my first crushes were almost all white boys. There was Jake Capella, my tall, lithe, athletic bully who was my main antagonist throughout middle and high school, but, what can I say, I love a challenge. I was obsessed with every inch of him. He had this protruding Adam's apple I would catch myself ogling during our classes together. Jake would always make fun of me, but not in as cruel a way as some of the other kids. But he was persistent. He would make fun of my weight or my glasses, but I secretly appreciated his attention. God, that explains so much of my dating life.

Jake loved coming up with nicknames for people, and because of his humor and force of personality, they often stuck, even if they initially seemed cruel. Our mutual friend Stefan became Buff because, Jake observed one day, his hair made him look like a buffalo. Dan became Sucio, Spanish for "dirty," because, Jake said, Dan's house was dirty. Once he learned my middle name was Fabian, Jake started calling me Pheebs, like Lisa Kudrow's character on *Friends*. I got off pretty easy, though Jake took every opportunity he could get to roast me. Sometimes I'd fire back, but I learned the best way to deal with him was just to laugh along. If we were both laughing, then I was in on the joke, and maybe Jake would like me more.

This was the same Jake about whom I wrote secret fan fiction and daydreamed. One day, I hoped, his animosity would turn to admiration. When Netflix's British dramedy *Sex Education* premiered in 2019 with its love story between the openly gay and Black Eric Effiong and his tall, lithe, athletic, and very white bully Adam Groff with his protruding Adam's apple, the sad fifteen-year-old faggot inside me that I will always be cried just a little. Or a lot.

When I first discovered "Smoke, Lilies and Jade," it came as both a relief (*Oh, Black boys have been pining after white boys for at least a century!*) and an indictment (*Oh . . . Black boys have been pining after white boys for at least a century . . .*). Nugent's love story was groundbreaking because it was queer and interracial at a time when both were taboo and/or illegal. There would be other gay stories and novels throughout the twentieth century, but very few with a Black protagonist, and very few that rapturously praised and exalted Black male beauty. Sure, there were copious references to big Black dicks scattered among the gay literary canon, but where was the rhapsodic, poetic appreciation evident in the books I devoured to get a better understanding of who I was and what I could be, of Black features, of Black skin, the napes of Black necks, of Black hair, eyelashes, and fingers?

James Baldwin came out with what many consider the greatest gay novel, *Giovanni's Room*, in 1956. Despite being authored by a Black gay writer—really, *the* Black gay writer— it's about two white boys. Baldwin later said that *Giovanni's Room* was too crowded as it was with the gay shit to bring in the Black shit: "I certainly could not possibly have—not at that point in my life—handled the other great weight, the 'Negro problem.' The sexual-moral light was a hard thing to deal with. I could not handle both propositions in the same book. There was no room for it."

It was 1956, so he had a point. Nugent didn't have to, or didn't feel the need to, handle the "Negro problem" with his scant short story, which is less about being Black and more about being a young artist in love. Baldwin would try to handle both "problems" in 1962's *Another Country*, though his Black queer protagonist (spoiler alert!) dies by suicide early on in the book and said protagonist's gay lovers are all exclusively white. And like his characters in *Giovanni's Room* and Alex in "Smoke, Lilies and Jade," Baldwin's queer male characters in *Another Country* are not gay but bisexual. As if Baldwin and Nugent were hesitant to go full-blown gay, something their white counterparts were less worried about, because, one assumes, they could be. Gore Vidal's *The City and the Pillar* came out in 1948, and its protagonist, Jimmy Willard, is a big old corn-fed all-American faggot. By the time he got to 1979's *Just Above My Head*, his sixth and final novel, Baldwin is still killing his Black gay darlings, but his protagonist, Arthur, doesn't hide under the slightly more respectable(?) guise of bisexuality, and he actually has love affairs with Black men.

Still, *Just Above My Head* isn't strictly a gay novel, just as *Another Country* isn't. Baldwin is more concerned with handling the great weight of American morality as it relates to Blackness, as it relates to queerness, but he could never be

Black or gay enough for everyone's taste. Eldridge Cleaver famously wrote of his dislike of *Another Country*, particularly its depiction of interracial homosexual desire, referring to it as a "racial death-wish" in his 1968 essay "Notes on a Native Son." Cleaver writes that "Negro homosexuals" are simply "frustrated" that they can't have babies with a white man and so they end up "bending over and touching their toes" for them, leading to "the unwinding of their nerves" and the further "intake of the white man's sperm."

Yeah, but, sis, I'm a top. What about the white man's intake of *my* sperm?

I'VE FALLEN IN love with so many white boys over the years. If not love, at least lust. It was never truly love—that remains elusive. But whenever I imagine myself in love, it's always with a white man. I've dated (read: slept with) men of all backgrounds because I'm an equal opportunity slut, but in my heart, I think I will, I want to, end up with a white man. And that thought has haunted me since its realization. Why wouldn't I want to fall in love with a Black man? Or any non-white man? Why does the ideal man of my dreams have to be of a certain race at all? I've had to interrogate my own desire and the immense guilt around it since I crushed on Jake Capella a quarter century ago. His very whiteness informed my perception of him, as my tormentor and oppressor, as something unattainable, as someone so unlike me in so many ways.

I used to think that my attraction to whiteness was a reflection of some inner self-loathing, but if I'm being honest, I've developed a *really* unhealthy obsession with myself. Like, a bitch has got it going on twelve ways from Sunday. This is, however, an act of overcompensation. If I don't believe that I'm, with all due respect to Trina, da baddest bitch, it's only a matter of time before I backslide into questioning if I'm even a worthwhile human being. I've struggled with accepting my Blackness like I think a lot of Black people in America have, especially when you're told, either implicitly or explicitly, through language or legislation, through history or an attempt at erasure of that history, that you're not good enough. Then to be queer on top of that is to invite even more of society's ire, to shoulder even more of the burden for the ills of the world, to feel as if your very presence is a blight on humanity. If you're not surrounded with any sort of counterprogramming—be it love or art or some sort of passion—you're likely to believe these lies told about you. As I got older, the culture around identity changed enough to provide some of that much-needed counterprogramming, but more important, I just got older.

As an adult, you have some agency, albeit very limited, in defining what life is and how you fit into it. By the time I got to that point, I had already been questioning everything, all the lies—so then I had to figure out what the truth was. I'm still figuring that out, but in the figuring out I've learned to love being Black, to love being gay, and to love the densely layered and beautifully textured nexus of both identities.

It's just really hard sometimes. A lot of the times. To be both, and not to feel enough of either. To not be Black enough for Black people, and to feel like an outsider among the gays, an outlier among those who should be your community, your peers, your family. No matter how comfortable I am in my own Blackness, I feel it will always be questioned, by both Black and white people, because I don't conform to a certain understanding of what a Black man is or should be. Black folks have their own ideal, and white folks theirs, and they are as different as night and the morning three weeks hence. I don't know where I fit into either of these archetypes, nor do I particularly care to fit into any archetype whatsoever.

I imagine myself getting a white boyfriend and secretly admonishing myself for being yet another Black boy living his little white-boy fantasy. But being with a white man would grant me a form of legitimacy among the gays, a social escort through the machinations of gay life with which I never felt comfortable in the first place. With my token white boy, I would be granted the legitimacy of existing in the same predominantly white and white-controlled spaces not as an intruder but as something more than a guest. (Though I would never make the mistake of believing that I actually belonged.) In dating a white boy, however, I would risk losing further legitimacy among Black people, gay or not—either in actuality or just in my own eyes.

Suspicion always follows a white person among Black people. Not so much hostility as a genuine wondering of *What's going on here, and who invited you?* So I'm not just worried about what everyone else thinks, and that's none of my business anyway. I worry about what I think of myself and what dating a white boy says about me. Am I not enough? Is my Blackness not enough? Am I betraying my race? Am I just another stereotype? The great weight, indeed. To be Black and gay is to have to deal with the implications of your desire. When all I've ever wanted was to be in love. Yet, love remains elusive because I keep it at bay, out of fear of my own desire. I shouldn't desire whiteness; therefore, I shouldn't have love.

A YEAR BEFORE the publication of *Just Above My Head*, four novels—gay novels—were published, making 1978 a watershed year in queer literature. The three most cited are Larry Kramer's *Faggots*, Edmund White's *Nocturnes for the King of Naples*, and my favorite of the triad, Andrew Holleran's *Dancer from the Dance*. Having recently read James Purdy's *Narrow Rooms*, I would also include that in the pantheon, above both Kramer and White, and perhaps even above Holleran. But they all prominently feature beautiful white boys in some capacity, either as protagonists or objects of desire or derision.

I first read *Dancer from the Dance* upon a friend's recommendation while visiting Provincetown, my homo away from home. My group of friends ended up reading it and loving it, its sweaty scenes of dancing in New York discos at all hours of the night and the capricious falling-in-love of summertime. Its colorful language and characters spoke to us, who fancied ourselves time-displaced faggots anyway. There was also the melancholy of it all, a sadness and tragedy that presaged the coming epidemic, and the loneliness that is a cornerstone of gay life, particularly in a city as populous as New York.

I loved *Dancer from the Dance*, but while it spoke to me, it also omitted me. Black characters were relegated to the sidelines, with little in the way of description or dialogue. The star of the show was a basic-ass white man, Malone. He's white, preppy. Everyone's in love with him; he's a Christ-like figure who sacrifices himself for the sake of love. Or something. I hated Malone. I hate white guys whom everybody wants. It doesn't seem fair, is all. When I have so much to offer, everyone is falling over themselves for an Abercrombie ad with a J.Crew wardrobe.

Malone falls in love with dark-eyed Puerto Rican boys on the streets of New York, always craving a love that doesn't feel possible in his world of discos and poppers and Fire Island jaunts. Despite Malone's popularity among the boys, his only friend, Sutherland, is actually the *real* star of the show, a flamboyant, eternally turbaned queen high on life and any number of drugs. Sutherland, however, is kinda racist. He refers to Black people as "dinge," exclaims "a guinea hasn't got a heart!," and opines that the "real lovers"—the ones who truly understand love—are WASPs like him and Malone.

Isn't that how it's always been, though? That white people are protagonists of most romantic stories? Even though Malone lusts after Puerto Rican boys, he himself remains the universal object of desire. And yet, he Virginia Woolfs himself and walks into the ocean, heartbroken and alone.

Around the time I read *Dancer from the Dance*, I read (also on a recommendation from a friend while in Ptown) 1988's *The Swimming-Pool Library* by Alan Hollinghurst, one of the first gay novels I discovered that discussed the beauty of Black men. William Beckwith, a real Malone type, is having an affair with a Black guy named Arthur. But being an insatiable slut, Will's fucking just about everybody. There's a particular scene Hollinghurst writes with a Black bodybuilder that led me to excuse myself with a box of tissues. Hollinghurst is interesting because his books often exalt white male beauty, particularly aristocratic white male beauty, but he also turns a lustful gaze to Black men and the working class.

Hollinghurst's *The Line of Beauty*, published in 2004, is hands down one of my favorite novels, if only for its preponderance of cocaine, and is a perfect example of this. Social climber Nick Guest falls for Leo, a Black boy, whom he meets in London through a personal ad. It's set in the Thatcherite '80s. Though I can't remember how he described it, I remember how I felt reading his description of the beauty of Leo's ass. All those years and all those books I read trying to understand what it was to be gay, how to be gay, what to gay-expect, all those beautiful white boys so lovingly described, their hair, their eyes, the napes of their necks, and I finally got some butt stuff.

Alan Hollinghurst is, importantly, British. Though the Brits may have invented racism, America sure as shootin' perfected it. For that very reason I tend to gravitate toward foreign men. I find their racism less offensive, even when it is blatantly obvious. Like, I never need to know that I'm your first time with a Black guy, but I can assume as much if you're from the whitest part of Europe. And Europe is white as hell. The racism of foreign white boys is rooted in an unwitting ignorance devoid of history or context. The racism of American white boys is rooted in the deliberate ignorance of history and context. And I can't fuck or fuck with deliberate ignorance. It's the difference between simply not knowing and not wanting or caring to know.

The religion of America is and always has been white supremacy. So when Eldridge Cleaver critiques *Another Country* and talks about Black characters submitting to a white man, he's talking about submitting to the White Man, to whiteness and all its history. I can't fully explain my desire, but I know it comes partially out of some unknown and unknowable quirk within me, and partially through the childhood socialization that normalized white supremacy. From my first days in America, I was assaulted with the American Dream: to be white; to be upwardly mobile; to be a consumer; to buy your life, your liberty, and your happiness. But no matter how much money you have, you can never buy whiteness.

Black people always joke that whenever a Black man gets any money, he almost immediately finds himself a white woman. It's funny because it's true. I know I side-eye Black men with white women, but to a Black woman with a white man, I quietly think, *Good for you, girl.* Because I want a white man. A white man represents my American Dream, my proximity to whiteness, whether consciously or unconsciously. My desire has been colonized under the motto "To be white is to be happy; to be happy is to be white." At the same time, in the same breath, I learned early on that to be gay is to be tragic; it is tragic to be gay. I was among the last generation where that was true, and it had been true for a whole-ass century, longer even.

Gays were notably visible in the '90s after being invisible for most of the century, but when I was a child, my view was limited to very sanitized versions. I think one of the most radical, subversive queer films ever made is *The Birdcage*. It's a big-budget, glitzy family comedy—starring *multiple* Oscar winners—about two men who love each other. The film challenges gender roles and the idea of the traditional family without sacrificing the jokes, for chrissakes. Jokes, people! Remember comedy?! With comedy you can afford to be radical. If anything, it's an obligation. *The Birdcage* was a positive representation of a queer relationship, of queer love, in a decade when the silver screen was obsessed with killing faggots and killer faggots. And in the center of the story, you had Robin Williams looking like a *snack* in Versace and Nathan Lane turning in the performance of the decade, endearing themselves to audiences. Not a kiss between them, but I guess we just weren't there yet.

Noxeema Jackson—you know, "Jesse's daughter"—was about the only Black gay character I remember seeing as a kid in a movie. I was too young for and not at all interested in Will Smith in *Six Degrees of Separation* . . . and that's about all I can recall of actual cinematic characters and not caricatures. There was always the comedic relief or sidekick who maybe had a good line or a funny facial expression, but Black gay characters were otherwise very few and very far between. What's interesting is that Noxeema, in the wonderfully tacky *To Wong Foo, Thanks for Everything! Julie Newmar*, was played by Wesley Snipes, at the time a symbol of Black male virility and power. And there he was, in a dress, serving if not fish, then perhaps canned tuna as Miss Jackson, if you're nasty. And what a performance! The comedic timing, the commitment, the nails. Snipes is, however, in drag for 99 percent of the movie. We get to see his bald man-head but once as he's getting dressed. So he's a gay man, but performing as and being mistaken for a woman.

But there were other gay white characters on film whose stories often, *Birdcage* notwithstanding, ended tragically. I was only five or six when *My Own Private Idaho* came out, but when I did finally see it, I fell in love with it. It was the kind of beautiful, aching, poetic gay love story I had read about in books and that I had imagined awaited me in life. I could cry thinking of the way River Phoenix struggles to tell Keanu Reeves he loves him while sitting by a campfire. I have cried many times at *Brokeback Mountain*, the way Heath Ledger snuggles against Jake Gyllenhaal's fucking perfect face like a puppy greeting a gravely missed owner, or later presses his face against the hanging coat of his dead lover.

Recently, I was high on shrooms and craving that poetic longing, so I turned to *God's Own Country*, a 2017 British film about two farmers who fall desperately in love. Like River Phoenix's Mike Waters or Heath Ledger's Ennis del Mar, Josh O'Connor's Johnny Saxby is a terse but immensely sensitive and impossibly beautiful loner awakened by the love of the devastatingly handsome and sincere Gheorghe Ionescu, a Romanian immigrant played by Alec Secăreanu who comes to work on Johnny's family farm. A passion writ large against a desolate, breathtaking countryside. Oh, all these beautiful white boys hopelessly in love, fucking each other's brains out in the great outdoors. All I want now is to own a farm on which to fuck a gorgeous, brooding man.

However, I only ended up watching *God's Own Country* because I couldn't find *Moonlight* streaming. The 2016 film, which famously snatched the Best Picture Oscar from *La La Land*'s overrated hands, was what I had been waiting for all my life. I sat through so much gay crap in my youth. There were a handful of tasteful outliers, though: One other faggy fave was 1985's *My Beautiful Laundrette* (has any human being ever been hotter than young Daniel Day-Lewis with a blond streak?). And I did love the Merchant Ivory 1987 production of *Maurice*, based on E. M. Forster's posthumously published novel of the same name, which, in 1913, when it was written, deigned to imagine a relatively happy ending for the titular gay character. Even though *My Beautiful Laundrette* concerned a gay, inter-racial relationship between Day-Lewis's street-tough Johnny and the more well-to-do Pakistani Omar and the beautiful launderette they manage together, nearly all the gay films I had seen were overwhelmingly white, focusing intently on the beauty of their white protagonists.

The late '90s, early '00s were full of so much soft-core gay porn masquerading, poorly, as films of sociopolitical import. LGBTQ+ films were important by their very existence, when we queers had to satisfy our urge to be seen with Mrs. Danvers from *Rebecca* or Norman Bates in *Psycho*. They were villains, loonies, and malcontents. So it was great to have examples of gays living ordinary-like lives, even if the men playing them had been plucked from the pages of underwear catalogs. And apparently Black people didn't wear underwear.

There were two types of queer films during this period when the doors of the celluloid closet had fallen off the hinges:

the prestige gay film and the trash gay film. The prestige films, your *Brokeback Mountains*, your *Capotes*, your *Bad Educations*, were by critically acclaimed directors with straight major stars who were often rewarded for their bravery in playing social pariahs with gilded trophies come Oscars season. The trash films, your *Tricks*, your *Eating Outs* one to five, David DeCoteau's entire oeuvre of homoerotic horror, were often indie or straight to video or DVD, and starring gorgeous white himbos for whom acting ability was rarely a requirement. Now, some people love *Trick* and think it's actually a good movie. Good for them. It is not, but I can't fault someone for loving something in which they finally feel seen.

All those films, prestige or trash or anywhere in between, served a function. I detest the phrase "representation matters," because like "woke," "diva," or "democracy," it doesn't mean anything anymore. "Representation matters" has become a parody of itself, the punch line to a bad show I'm supposed to like because it stars the first queer person of color named Chad in a supporting role. But it is important to feel seen. I didn't see myself in these films or in these books, not that there weren't versions of me around. The documentaries *Tongues Untied* and, of course, *Paris Is Burning* painted pictures of Black queer life. E. Lynn Harris wrote about the lives and loves of Black queer men, but I just couldn't get into him. I tried reading one of his books and was immediately put off by the bad writing.

As much as I hungered for representation, I've always known representation doesn't matter if it's not of quality. Harris authored fifteen books, many of them bestsellers, just as Tyler Perry, often a purveyor of homoerotic and homophobic sentiment himself, has made a slew of commercially successful films and plays. So clearly someone likes them. That someone, however, is not me. Had Harris, and Perry for quite a while, not been the only game in town—both canons unto themselves—I might not have found their predominance so disappointing.

But they opened doors. They paved ways. They made things like *Moonlight* possible.

Tarell Alvin McCraney wrote the nontraditional play *In Moonlight Black Boys Look Blue* in 2003 as an "experiment in what life could look like." He had just lost his mother to complications from AIDS and was filled with questions—about himself, about life, about going out into the world—that he could no longer turn to his mother to answer. Neither a traditional stage script or screenplay, *In Moonlight* served as a "circular map" for McCraney, a way to locate himself, socially and historically.

"I was very afraid of what my life would look like," McCraney told me when I interviewed him for *Out* in 2016. "I was very lonely. I still feel very alone most of the time and so I tried to figure out and put down as much of the memory that I could."

He continued to rework and revisit *In Moonlight*, then, along with director Barry Jenkins, wrote the screenplay for one of the most lauded films of this century. A story about a gay Black boy, his complicated relationship with his mother, a father figure lost to violence, and a young love pure and innocent against so much misery and pain. Trevante Rhodes played the eldest version of the protagonist, Chiron. And he is beautiful. A beautiful, complicated, sad (I prefer my gays melancholy)

Black boy as the object of attraction, as the focal point, and not a white boy in sight.

As a kid, Chiron is bullied relentlessly by other kids at school and by his drug-addicted mother at home. His only reprieve is his relationship with his mom's dealer, Juan, one complicated by Juan's role in the downfall of Chiron's mother, but Juan is the only father figure in his life. When Juan is murdered, Chiron finds an unexpected connection with his childhood friend Kevin, with whom he shares a moonlit kiss (and god bless those kids, a discreet handjob) on the beach. It was a kiss that meant a world of unexplored possibilities for both of them, and when they are reunited years later, it's as two halves becoming whole. A passion writ large against the Miami projects.

In a way, Tarell Alvin McCraney finished what Richard Bruce Nugent had started ninety years prior, but with a very important caveat: not presenting Black queer desire through an interracial lens. So often, too often—like, almost always—gay Black men cannot exist in representations in the media without the interference or permission of a white gatekeeper, as if the presence of whiteness justifies their existence.

Besides *Moonlight*, another notable exception is *Noah's Arc*, a groundbreaking dramedy about four friends in the rigid mold of *Sex and the City*. *Noah's Arc* had its share of faults, but at least it was fun and sexy, if melodramatic and rife with clichés. And truly questionable outfits. So many terrible hats and random, seasonally inappropriate scarves—Carrie Bradshaw really was a plague on fashion in the early aughts.

Moonlight itself didn't change anything, but it was part of a new sort of renaissance, one of art and thought and culture spurred by the historically marginalized, ushered in by social media and Black Twitter and by the first (and, at this rate, only) Black president. The arts are always a barometer of not necessarily where a society is at but where it's going. I felt this sea change; it was vibrant and, in immediate retrospect, rapid, but in the grand scheme of things, it was also a long time coming. More than a hundred years, something like four hundred. And yet, the people holding the reins of power remained mostly the same.

When *Moonlight* won Best Picture, the three people who won the actual Oscar, the producers of the film, were all white. But at least two of them were women . . . progress! For some. For Black people, it seems we still need a white escort to lend us legitimacy in this white-controlled world. I mean, god bless well-meaning white people for raising money, opening doors, and *allowing* Black people to control our own narratives. Not that we needed or asked for permission.

An episode of the second season of *Harlem*, a dramedy about four Black gals living their best life in the titular neighborhood, revolves around New York's annual messy, shirtless white-boy parade, Pride. Quinn, a bougie try-hard trying to figure out who she is, has recently come out as bisexual and is excited for her first Pride. Tye, a self-possessed and sexually promiscuous stud, has no intention of going, citing the messy, shirtless whiteness previously stated. But being a good friend, Tye acquiesces and goes to Pride, where she's almost immediately assaulted by a drunk white gay trying to touch her boobs, using that old adage "It's okay, I'm gay." Elsewhere, Angie and her on-again, off-again bisexual fuck buddy Eric also entertain going to Pride but then turn against the idea as neither of them are fans of "shirtless white guys" either. I thought how lucky they must be. *Harlem* is such a pro-Black, pro-queer show in which white people exist as foils and caricatures, the same reductive way Black people have always existed in white shows and movies. The world of *Harlem* is a world that is not infatuated with whiteness. And how lucky those characters must be to live in such a world.

I've often thought my life would be simpler, happier, even, if I wasn't attracted to white guys. It's such an unnecessary complication. I wouldn't go so far as Cleaver to call it a racial death-wish, but it is an active way to court heartache. The persistent heartache of knowing that racism exists in all corners of society, in every manner of white man, even the gay ones . . . some might say especially the gay ones. I have to preface my attraction with the inner query *Are you into Black guys?* I've envied Black boys who didn't have my same affliction. And I wondered how they escaped the indoctrination. How did they decolonize their desire? Because my infatuation with whiteness is just a logical extension of the society in which I live. America is infatuated with whiteness. Particularly with white men. They're the founders, the leaders, the heroes, the pillars of American virtue, truth, justice, whatever, etc., and who cares. The idea of white men, if not a white man devoid of context, is appealing. Even the most basic white man stands taller, shines brighter, takes up more space through his whiteness. But that's just because whiteness diminishes, and dims, and takes and takes and takes from everything not white. It's the loudest voice in the room because it's shouting over everyone. So how could I tune it out?

I could neither ignore whiteness nor avoid being seduced by it. Whiteness represented so much of what I wanted out of this American life. Freedom, prosperity, power, access, legitimacy. Fucking white boys became, perhaps unconsciously, a way of claiming those things for myself. Yes, there was the obvious attraction, but there's more to the dynamic within interracial queer relationships than attraction, because they don't exist in a vacuum. I don't exist in a vacuum. I can't pretend that being gay in this world doesn't make me a target and being a Black man doesn't make me a perceived threat. I could have just been seeking refuge in white boys even though, or because, they could never understand my particular predicament.

But then there's the burden of having to explain, the burdens of microaggressions and misunderstandings that would no doubt crush any relationship under their insurmountable weight. I could just hold out for some virtuous white man who would need no explaining and, thank the heavens, also feel no need to explain to me the intricacies of racism. Holding out for a hero, holding out for a savior, just a ripped, blue-eyed, anglicized, flowing-hair Jesus Christ fresh off the cross come to take me away from all this . . . reality.

To truly decolonize my desire, I would first have to decolonize how I see the world. Because it's not like I can decolonize the world itself. That would require an act of universal human cooperation. My worldview is one predicated on the indoctrinated belief in white supremacy. It's what I've been taught—implicitly and explicitly, through language and legislation, through history and an attempt at erasure of that history—since I set foot in this country or maybe even before. There aren't a lot of white folks in Guyana, but until 1966, it was a colony of, like so many of the darker parts of the globe, Great Britain. Since its decolonization, Guyana has struggled to find its place in the world. Beset by poverty, governmental instability, predatory nations, and predatory white men—lest we forget good ole Jim Jones. But Guyana is still an autonomous nation, free to determine its own future, separate from the past.

My own freedom is conditional. I'm no slave to my desire. I'm just highly annoyed by it. I'm troubled by it. I'm anxious about it. I'm resentful of it. I'm tremendously guilty over it. I'm wary of it. And, moreover, I'm weary of it. I'm weary of writing about white boys, weary of reading about them, weary of watching white boys fall in and out of love, weary of falling in and out of love with white boys who don't love me. I'm weary of romanticizing whiteness. Like, can a dude just fuck another dude the way god intended—high on poppers and devoid of racial constructs?

But whiteness has proven itself inescapable in my life—in American life, really—and so have white boys. I wish I didn't have as much guilt, as much resentment and anger, about my attraction to them, but how can I not? How can I be a Black man in America and not resent whiteness?

The other, more important question is: Why should I feel guilty? What the hell did I do but experience the world in the way I did? And maybe try to occasionally get my dick wet.

Perhaps if I had had more *Moonlights* growing up, I wouldn't fetishize whiteness so much—but then again, perhaps not. It would have been nice, though, to have had the option, to be able to see and read about and thus romanticize Black gay men tenderly in love, rather than always having to deal with fucking white boys.

2

I WORSHIP AT THE ALTAR OF HIS BODY

THERE'S NOTHING QUITE like injecting steroids into your ass to make you really question your life choices.

In 2013, the American Psychiatric Association recognized muscle dysmorphia in its fifth edition of the *Diagnostic and Statistical Manual of Mental Disorders*, classifying it as a subtype of body dysmorphia, another obsessive mental disorder. I wrote about my own self-diagnosed battles with muscle dysmorphia three years later, having come upon the definition on some random day on the internet.

I'm always trying to figure out, as I've been asked numerous times, what the hell is wrong with me. That is, why I feel a certain way about things or about myself. The search for the answer yielded "muscle dysmorphia," a chronic sense of muscular inadequacy. Gay men are particularly susceptible to muscle dysmorphia and steroid use for any number of reasons: internalized heterosexism; internalized beauty standards;

homophobic bullying; long-term effects of the AIDS epidemic, both physical and psychological; and just the constant pressure (and competition) to be seen, to be wanted, to be fucked.

Though I was a chubby little gay kid, I had a secret love all my own. The first time I saw bodybuilding on television, I was shocked that it was a real thing. Beautiful, jacked men, all oiled up in tiny briefs, posing and flexing next to one another on a stage? What gay sorcery is this? Like, point me to the genius faggot who came up with the idea to call this a sport so I can vigorously shake his hand.

Later I discovered that faggot would most likely be noted heterosexual Eugen Sandow, often credited as the "father of modern bodybuilding" (and all-around daddy) in whose image the statue for the most prestigious title in bodybuilding, Mr. Olympia, is modeled. The statue itself is known as the Sandow, and among its winners is Arnold Schwarzenegger, who won the title seven times before becoming an international movie star.

Idolatry of the male physique goes back to at least the ancient Greeks, the first muscle kweens in civilized history. The Greeks created an ideal that Sandow intentionally followed for himself, down to the exact measurements, and that subsequent generations have imitated and surpassed, reaching levels of musculature through rigorous dieting, advanced training techniques, and a sometimes lethal combination of drugs. All this, to achieve a statue in Sandow's name and likeness—or just to appear statue-like. Sandow founded the first bodybuilding mag, *Physical Culture*, in 1898 and presented the first bodybuilding show in 1901. The event was a respectable affair, with Sandow serving as a judge alongside Sir Arthur Conan Doyle.

That bodybuilding has such staunchly heterosexual roots came as a big old shock to me, but it didn't take long for the queer eye to find the straight guy. Popular in the '40s through the '60s, physique or beefcake magazines featuring oiled-up Adonises wearing next to nothing and executing Grecian poses were marketed to, and often created by, gay men. This all under the respectable guise of being magazines about health and fitness. Actually, if there's any faggot's hand that needs a good shaking, it's Bob Mizer's. If Sandow is the father of bodybuilding, Mizer is the daddy of bodybuilding photography.

A 2016 *New Yorker* profile referred to him as "a tireless collector of physical specimens." Same. Mizer photographed more than ten thousand men, including a young Schwarzenegger, many appearing in the pages of *Physique Pictorial*, which he founded in 1951. *Physique Pictorial* was considered basically the first gay magazine. He took the premise of Sandow's *Physical Culture* but freed his models from rigid bodybuilding poses against boring backdrops. Instead, he turned them into glorious pinups in Greco-Roman settings, adorned in tiny posing outfits allegedly sewn by his mother.

Mizer sold homoerotic imagery as wholesome entertainment, but that gay sorcery wasn't fooling everybody. In 1954, a Los Angeles court found him guilty of selling "indecent literature," with his wrestling photos described as "scenes of brutality and torture." Mizer's studio was raided, and he was arrested and sentenced to two months in jail, but following an appeal, the judgment was overturned the following year. *Physique Pictorial* also included homoerotic art by the likes of Tom of Finland, whose drawings of buff, rough tradesmen in blue-collar jobs came to embody a certain gay aesthetic. The lines between bodybuilding and homosexuality continued to blur.

Mizer didn't limit his lens to bodybuilders alone, including hustlers and porn stars, as well as future Hollywood stars like Tab Hunter, himself a closeted gay. "Homosexuality was the standard way of life among the rugged Greek warriors," Mizer wrote in a 1960 issue of *Physique Pictorial*. "Bodybuilding, and the creation of a rugged powerful body, will almost always remove the stigma of 'sissy' from a young man." This tacit understanding or relationship between bodybuilding culture and gay culture, remains something of an open secret today.

Bodybuilding is also incredibly expensive, and though it has a level of popularity, its following can't match that of other sports, where star athletes get lucrative seven- and eight-figure deals for product endorsements. Bodybuilding is very much a sport of passion, not profit, so the truly dedicated often turn to other means of financial support, and gay men are their primary patrons. Whether it's escort work, stripping, or go-going; appearing in muscle-play videos or porn; or more modern avenues like OnlyFans, there's always a market for beautiful, muscular men, and the audience is almost exclusively gay men. Another popular source of spare income is paid muscle worship, where a bodybuilder poses, maybe naked, maybe not, for an adoring fan, who shells out hundreds if not thousands of dollars for the pleasure of their company.

I've not only considered paying for this but have also been solicited for those very services. Honestly, the way my love life is going, paying for escorts or bodybuilders to worship sounds much easier than dating. Hell, I'd be paying for it now if I had the dollars. Skipping the pain and heartbreak and relentless disappointment of hookup apps and cutting straight to the best part, my favorite part, feeling up on some titties? That's a no-brainer.

As for being on the other side of those titties, I will say I've enjoyed the times I've been worshipped, but I'm just not personally comfortable with the idea of selling my body, not with the centuries of ownership of Black bodies at my back, not to mention the fetishization and exploitation of the Black male body. That, and I really don't like being touched by strangers unless they're providing me with a raging hard-on—it's a fair trade.

But I digress. Despite this symbiosis between faggots and bodybuilding, the sport is fueled by testosterone, both naturally occurring and injected, which in turn fuels a Darwinian fixation on being an "alpha," a he-man among men, top dog, the biggest dick swingin' in these parts of the wood, or what have you. Masculinity is a god, and these alphas mold themselves in his image. This religious devotion to masculinity can then result in the rejection of anything that might deflate the appearance of their pumped-up, rippling manliness in the eyes of their fellow gym acolytes.

And the rejection of anything that may whiff of, oh, I don't know, being a faggot. So even while stoking homoerotic fervor and benefiting from those pink dollars, some bodybuilders adopt a homophobic stance. Perhaps they doth protest too much, but you'd think dudes who flaunt their ass cheeks in public might have a bit more security in their manhood. Or then again, maybe not. Bodybuilding is all about the beauty of the human body, so does coveting and complimenting the beauty of another man immediately spark within some men a fear of their own homosexuality? Does devoting so much time and money to one's physical appearance somehow undermine the very rigid definition of what makes a man? I'm gonna go out on a limb here and say, "Duh."

But the definition of manliness, while rigid, does change, however slightly, from generation to generation. I feel we're living in a true golden age of the male peacock.

WHEN BOB MIZER was taking his beefcake photos, he was trying to recapture the beauty of men that had been celebrated by the ancient Greeks and then taken up again by those lewd and lascivious Renaissance artists who carved all those sculpted male buttocks and painted those chiseled male torsos. When, then, did men stop being beautiful? Even when Eugen Sandow stripped down to his banana leaf in yet another attempt at re-creating the Grecian ideal centuries after the Renaissance, was he considered beautiful? Or was his body just an achievement to be marveled at but not sexually desired by anyone? Certainly not other men. Of course, women didn't have sexual desires back then, at least none acknowledged by society.

Sandow's physique was so impressive, though, that he was the subject of several short films at the dawn of this new technology. Film awakened a new type of sexuality, one more overt, larger than life, and in glorious black and white. Into this brave, horny new world tangoed Rudolph Valentino, the first male beauty icon of the twentieth century. Though no Sandow, Valentino appeared working out shirtless in publicity stills and bared his chest in the 1924 film *Monsieur Beaucaire*. Though women loved him, men reviled Valentino, thinking him effeminate. Men were more apt to be inspired by the far less handsome—but more traditionally masculine—swashbuckling Douglas Fairbanks.

Decades later, the image of a male movie star, nipples out, inspires mass swooning. We now have superhero films and actors getting into super-heroic shape. As soon as anyone is announced for a new high-flying cinematic adventure, the countdown begins for the first glimpses of the newly buff beefcake. Actors regularly graduate to a new level of stardom thanks in part to these transformations. Yes, it's part of the gig, doing stunts and executing elaborate fight choreography, but there are also the aesthetics to consider. Superheroes, in their tight-fitting, muscle-bulging costumes and *dramatic* capework, have been making little boys gay for decades, so much so that famed stick-in-the-mud Dr. Fredric Wertham wrote a book about it, *Seduction of the Innocent*, in 1954.

In it, Wertham claims that comic books have a corrupting influence on children and that Batman condoned homosexuality since he and Robin were clearly lovers. Anyone who has seen Joel Schumacher's 1997 queer shlock masterpiece *Batman & Robin*, or *Saturday Night Live*'s still-hilarious Robert Smigel cartoon *The Ambiguously Gay Duo*, knows Wertham wasn't too far off. Meanwhile, the Marvel Cinematic Universe has become a veritable hunk factory, churning out buff Chris after buff Chris to lead blockbuster after blockbuster, so by this point if anyone showed up with less than a six-pack, they might as well get off the fucking soundstage.

Though women have had to deal with an entire century of being objectified on film, the degree to which men are now exposed to this same kind of objectification, which still pales in comparison to their female counterparts, creates the same kind of insecurity for both the star and the audience that consumes his beauty. Former teen heartthrob Zac Efron sent heads turning and wrists pounding when he got super-jacked for the otherwise unwatchable *Baywatch* movie. Since then, he's been very clear that he never wants to be that ripped again, calling the shape he got into "unrealistic" and that he didn't want to "glamorize" it.

Kumail Nanjiani, known previously as a comic actor, got seriously jacked for 2021's *The Eternals*, and his Instagram photos of his transformation went viral. He later told *GQ* that he found that talking about his body made him "less and less comfortable." Because it's as if now that's all people can think of when they look at him. Still, that was part of his original intent. He wanted to change the way *Hollywood* looked at him, a brown-skinned South Asian man.

While Nanjiani didn't even have any shirtless scenes in *Eternals*, sadly, and while director Chloé Zhao hadn't asked him to get ripped as fuck, he still found it necessary to do so. He wanted to get jacked both for his character and what he, Nanjiani, represented. "If I'm playing the first South Asian superhero, I want to look like someone who can take on Thor or Captain America, or any of those people," Nanjiani said. His *Eternals* character is also a Bollywood star, and having grown up with those movies and those jacked heroes, Nanjiani wanted to feel "believable" and "powerful" in the role.

Still, he was wary of the sort of masculinity associated with his type of physique and how his body inspires aggression in the "Do you even lift, bro?" kind of man. "A lot of times we are taught to be useful by using physical strength . . . in an aggressive, competitive way," Nanjiani continued. "And that's what the male ideal has been. Dominating. Defeating. Crushing. Killing. Destroying. That's what being jacked is."

The thing with this whole alpha male concept, however, is that it also correlates to gay sexual proclivities: as in a relationship between an alpha and a beta, a dom (dominant) and a sub (submissive). Being a homosexual doesn't preclude one from being an alpha, especially since gay men are equally, if not even more, susceptible to the intoxicating musk of masculinity. But it's kinda hilarious that in their attempts to further distance themselves from anything remotely gay, these so-called alphas are further playing into gay stereotypes.

I understand all too well the conflicting emotions Nanjiani expressed. Especially being a minority and wanting to be viewed or treated differently, and how that suddenly happens when you look a certain way, but then a whole new set of troubles arises. And the old troubles don't go away; they simply get bigger and louder. I often feel invisible in the gay community. It's why I avoid gay bars or clubs, as any sort of traditionally "safe space" feels anything but for me. And while I hate the apps, there's a certain safety in knowing that I can find men who are attracted to me. As RuPaul has warned queen after queen not to do, I began relying on that body-ody-ody.

The more I worked out, the more attention I got; the more attention I got, the more I worked out. I wanted to be unignorable, to never feel invisible again. But that's not how it works. I realized soon enough that it didn't matter how "hot" I was or thought I was—I would never be attractive to everyone, for whatever reason. So I decided that I should work out for myself, not for other men. They would never fully appreciate the work I put in, but I would. I would know the hours spent in the gym, the constant aches and pains, the sacrifices, the indulgences, the means I would justify for the ends. And if I did drink the bodybuilding Kool-Aid, which is hopefully laced with human growth hormone, I would need a better reason than simply getting laid. Though, let me be as clear and queer as possible, the getting-laid part was also pretty damn cool.

But for me, bodybuilding went deeper than sexual desire, which, again, super cool. I started collecting action figures when I was very young. I would fondle their hard, plastic torsos, getting aroused by having them display their strength against one another. When I say "as queer as possible," I'm not kidding, kids. I've had a pretty definite sense of who I am from about the age of four or five, when I first came to America and fell in love with the men on *American Gladiators* and pro wrestling. My family happened to love the then WWF, now the WWE, after the World Wildlife Fund came for its coins. One of my first memories of America is the Ultimate Warrior versus Hulk Hogan at WrestleMania VI on April 1, 1990. At four years old, I had been in the country since only January. And there I was, gay.

I loved the Ultimate Warrior, thinking him far more

attractive than the bloated-looking Hulk Hogan. When the Ultimate Warrior hoisted all 250 pounds of Hulkamania above his head, my tiny heart skipped a beat. God bless America. I thought this desire was wrong, even then, but my family, Hulkamaniacs some of them, enjoyed the spectacle, too. So my rabid attention was okay. Sanctioned fandom, even though they didn't know about my underlying lust.

From there I became fascinated with musculature and everywhere I could find it: superheroes in comic books, bodybuilding on TV and in magazines, workout shows on weekday mornings. The happiest times of my youth were the very special episodes, very special to me, in which a teen heartthrob hunk would doff his shirt, to the whoops and hollers of the audience. Joey Lawrence, an early childhood crush, had his shirt "accidentally" ripped off by a young Brittany Murphy (may she rest) on the short-lived NBC sitcom *Almost Home*, his voluminous pecs leaving both Brittany and me in awe. And then there was Mario Lopez, the hunky AC Slater from *Saved by the Bell*, who curls his massive biceps in the opening credits. God, that man could fill out a wrestling singlet. Still can, and I still would.

I liked to draw, and my main subjects were the X-Men, girls in pretty gowns, and, more and more as I grew older, jacked dudes. Some of them were versions of me. I studied anatomy books and how-to books on comic book drawing and developed a real ability to render the male human body in all its beauty. Could never quite get hands down, though. On shopping trips with my mom, I would sneak off in the grocery store checkout line or at the mall bookstore to pore over the pages of bodybuilding rags like *Muscular Development*, *Flex*, and *Mus-*

cle & Fitness. Once I was in high school and old enough to buy them on my own, I cut out the most appealing men and hid them in various shoeboxes under my bed. I shed a tear when I had to throw away all my men when I went to college. But by then there was the internet, and I never needed a shoebox again.

I had CDs and external hard drives full of muscular men archived for my future perusal, if such a time ever came. And it rarely did. I liked to collect—no, hoard, definitely hoard—images and videos of rippling physiques. I say "hoard" because I would have devoured the entire internet if I could have, so insatiable was my appetite for muscle and the men who possessed it. "A tireless collector of physical specimens."

Maybe I believed if I collected enough of these men, I could fill the void inside me that wanted to both possess them in the flesh and look like them in my own flesh. So when I started seriously bodybuilding, it was with these two goals in mind: possession and transformation. For a time, both were equally intoxicating and addictive, but possession inevitably lost its novelty.

THERE ARE TWO cycles in bodybuilding: bulking and cutting. In one, you ostensibly get to stuff your face, with varying parameters, and in the other, you ostensibly starve yourself, again, with varying parameters. I've never competed in a bodybuilding show, though the urge has been there since I was a kid drooling over *MuscleSport USA* on cable on Saturday afternoons. I've only bulked and cut on my own terms, in my quest to attain my ideal physique. I find both cycles difficult and enjoyable. When I'm bulking, I worry about eating enough, and I get anxiety just by looking at a plate of food because I'm not sure if I'll be able to finish it. And if I end up getting too fat, a "dirty bulk," my self-esteem plummets as my waistline balloons.

After I tore my ACL and gained forty pounds, I had to come to a different relationship with my body, which had never betrayed me and had done most of what I had asked. To its detriment. But I was also more determined than ever to get back into shape, no matter the cost. So I decided to finally do steroids. It felt like an inevitable decision. Steroids, like all drugs, had a dangerous stigma around them when I was growing up. They were something that "winners" didn't do, that is, until we found out that a particular winner failed a piss test. Still, steroids felt like something you did in the competitive arena, but back then I didn't realize how competitive being gay could be. Or how many gay men do or have done steroids, just casually.

My decision to start stickin', however, came from my own perception of my body image. The muscle dysmorphia. I knew I was getting older and that my testosterone levels would start to decrease, making it harder to build and maintain muscle. I knew I had gone through a pretty big surgery and wasn't losing weight as fast as I would've liked, and I knew that I wanted to achieve the physical ideal that had always haunted and taunted me for years, and time felt like a gift. I tore my ACL during the pandemic, when the rug had been pulled out from under the entire world, so why not just do the damn drugs? What did I have to lose?

Well, a lot, potentially, but tomorrow wasn't guaranteed and I wanted what I wanted. And I already had some steroids in storage. I had originally gotten them right before the pandemic, when 2020 was going to be MY YEAR! I was going to finally compete in a bodybuilding show, checking that lifelong dream off the list, and I serendipitously found a connection when I fucked this muscle daddy personal trainer. While he was riding my dick, he commented how I would look better with more muscle. I didn't take it personally—I felt the same way—but it did make me not want to see him again. But then we got to talking about steroids and he said he could get me some, so, of course, I had to see the motherfucker again. After sitting through some convoluted tale about how he took edibles and crashed his car into a pole and now he was riding a bike, this daddy gave me a vial of tren (trenbolone), one of the most powerful steroids on the market, and a vial of testosterone, to be taken together. It cost $200. He showed me how to inject myself and sent me on my way.

I only did the cycle for three weeks before the world shut down, but in that time, my right shoulder looked slightly deformed from the drugs. I didn't know what the hell I was doing, but I kept doing it until the gyms closed, and when they did, I put the rest of the roids away until I would be ready to lift again. Then my accident happened, working out in the park, not at the gym, with no weights involved. To think fucking nature would be my undoing.

After I had my surgery and had gone through physical rehab,

I was still overweight but even more determined to get from the worst shape of my life to the best. With some more research and asking around, mostly other gays who did steroids, I dug out my old vials and shot them up, one on the left side, one on the right, alternating between my ass and my thighs. The shoulders were more of a last resort, with the first two body parts being preferred, or so I gathered. I know I'll never get used to shooting myself with a needle; it's one of the reasons I've never done heroin—that and Mom prefers uppers—but I could imagine doing this for the rest of my life, or at least until I stopped lifting.

Roid rage is a real thing, but when you're already filled with rage, it's hard to tell the difference. My rage is actually one of the main reasons I work out. Lifting heavy things helps me channel my rage into something less destructive than, say, throwing my phone into my TV set, breaking both. Which I did once . . . at least once. In fact, I was working out my rage when I tore my ACL. Some boy on the apps had disappointed me by whatever-who-cares and I was thrusting myself up into the air with extra force while doing jump squats. On wet grass. On my third rep I landed incorrectly, heard a pop, and long story short, I'll never be able to drop it like it's hot again. But for years I dealt with rejection, and the attendant rage, by simply working out harder. To be unignorable, unrejectable. Yes, I was working out mostly for myself, but never just for myself. I still valued the attention I received from other men. And I still felt like that fat kid drawing muscular men alone in my room. I never felt enough.

When I worked out and my hard-won results were admired, I didn't feel so inadequate. Ironically, working out made me more calm, not more aggressive. There was a level of Zen-like enlightenment I could reach during workouts, a sense of inner peace I rarely found outside of doing shrooms. Even on steroids, when my aggression might go a bit unchecked, I can still find peace. Do I sometimes want to hurl a dumbbell into a mirror if someone is hogging a machine I need? Sure, I'm only human. But I don't, and that's what matters. I wouldn't dare defile such a sacred place.

The gym is sometimes referred to humorously as gay church, and not just because you have men sucking each other in private stalls (the Catholic church be wildin'). And I do go there to pray. My own form of prayer, to commune with my inner spirit. The gym is my one true safe space. I never feel any sort of fixation on becoming an alpha male, even when I know (to my great self-satisfaction) that I'm bigger and stronger than most of the guys in my gym, because I also know that I am a *faggot*. Like, more likely than not, at any given point while at the gym, I'm blasting "The Schuyler Sisters" from *Hamilton*. I don't even like *Hamilton* that much, but it's three big-voiced Broadway gals belting "WORK!" at me. I'm not trying to out-butch anyone, henny.

While I don't feel the need to prove my masculinity, being bigger and stronger than everyone else makes me feel safer being a faggot. Like many an effeminate overweight boy, I suffered my fair share of bullying, though I've never indulged in the fantasy of beating up my old tormentors, mostly because I'm just not a violent person, and no one laid a hand on my gentle, tubby behind. But simply passing through the world as a gay man, I'm emboldened by my own physical presence, this armor forged from countless hours in the gym. My body, then, is an instrument of attraction and deflection. Because of my stature, I can't imagine toxically masc bros wanting to step to me. Still, I'm all too aware of the ongoing danger of violence.

Black men are already perceived to be larger and stronger than white men, and thus are perceived as posing a greater threat, according to a 2017 study published by the American Psychological Association. While that may be great for my sex life, it puts my actual life in danger should a police officer consider me a greater threat than I am, as too many Black men have had to find out too often in this country. My body can at once make me feel safe and make me a target. With this bias already in place, if I got into a fight—and again, never have been—that I didn't start but had every intention of finishing, I could shoulder the totality of the blame for the altercation. It's easier to just walk away from some dick being a dick, especially since I have nothing to prove.

After my first full cycle in 2022, the side effects felt worth it for the results. I had successfully resculpted my body in the image I desired, better than I had looked before, but once I did, I only wanted more. To be bigger, to be more ripped. But bodybuilding, if you're serious about it, is a full-time occupation, and though it may look like an individual sport, there's a team of people behind most competitive bodybuilders. At the very least a coach and a bodywork specialist to work out the kinks and pains from destroying your joints and muscles on a regular basis. To get the way I want to look, I can't do it alone; I can't do it naturally. But what are the limits?

Bodybuilding has never been about health, just the appearance of superhuman physicality, and that is often pursued through the least healthy methods. Yet for men of any sexual orientation, the draw of all that rippling muscle is too strong to ignore. The last few years have been more concerned with "aesthetics"—conditioning, "shredz," etc.—over sheer size, but that movement was itself inspired by the death of a Russian-born Australian bodybuilder, Aziz Shavershian, aka Zyzz.

Starting with a series of YouTube videos in 2007, Zyzz became the poster boy of the aesthetics subculture that started in Australia but would spread like overdeveloped lats through social media. He claimed he started bodybuilding to impress girls, that he would look at pictures of shredded bodybuilders and tell himself that one day he would look like them. Except for the girls part, I had a similar origin story, having stared longingly at the divine muscles of mortal men with the aspiration that one day I, too, would look like that. Zyzz also described transcending the approval of women and relishing the "skin-tearing pumps" from working out and the unparalleled accomplishment of setting a goal, achieving it, and then outdoing oneself. Much like Zyzz, I soon found a joy and a passion in bodybuilding that superseded any attention I got from boys. That pump is as good as any high, but all highs can be destructive, even in the guise of health.

Though Zyzz denied using steroids—it's an open yet still dirty secret in bodybuilding that pretty much everyone uses them, at least when it comes to those achieving certain performance levels—his brother was arrested in July 2011 for possession of anabolic steroids. A month later, Zyzz was dead.

He suffered a heart attack in a sauna while on vacation, an autopsy later revealing he had an undiagnosed congenital heart defect. He was twenty-two. With his death, however, Zyzz became a martyr for the cult of bodybuilding, and for years following his death, young men repeated his hair, his wardrobe, and, increasingly, his mantra of aesthetics. His name is still invoked in Instagram posts and on tank tops, the Narcissus myth made legend.

Zyzz was hardly the first or the last bodybuilder to die in the pursuit of their passion. There has been a spate of deaths in the bodybuilding community documented in the last few years, among all genders, that's gone mostly overlooked because bodybuilding straddles the line between sport and art without being accepted by either. Only in 2022 did *The Washington Post* run a story on the deadly methods used to achieve impossible physiques, with a report that investigated the deaths of more than two dozen bodybuilders, shedding light on an industry rife with illegal drugs and a mentality of "get big or die trying" enabled by coaches, bodybuilding judges, and the athletes themselves.

That article really made me rethink whether I wanted to compete, because I know how I am. If I'm going to compete, I'm going to fucking win. But as an ambivalent hypochondriac, I often fear the worst when it comes to my health, but don't really care much to pursue whatever that might be. All those descriptions of beautiful bodies collapsing at their peak made me question but not stop my own steroid use. I believe in moderate, responsible drug use; I always have.

The Drug Enforcement Administration, however, does not, and its war on drugs has been a massive failure as folks are still out here getting addicted to and dying from various drugs. Not to mention the violence associated with the illicit drug trade. Congress passed the Anabolic Steroids Control Act of 1990 and redoubled its efforts in 2014 with the Designer (*ooooh!*) Anabolic Steroid Control Act. Prohibition has never and will never work. Regulation, however, proves far more effective in keeping people safe. It's the same with alcohol, or cocaine, or steroids. It's a victory if people aren't whipping up bathtub gin or formulating their own steroid compounds, because prohibiting a drug won't stop anyone from creating their own or seeking other illicit methods, which often prove more dangerous than the drugs themselves.

Steroids are necessary to keep up with the extreme bodies currently prevalent in the sport, and it's this extremity that keeps bodybuilding from going more mainstream. The bodies of today are insane compared to the so-called classic era of bodybuilding, when it was at its height in popularity—the '70s. Bodybuilding's zenith was the 1977 documentary *Pumping Iron*, following Arnold Schwarzenegger, Lou Ferrigno, and other classic-era icons such as Franco Columbu, Mike Katz, and Serge Nubret on their roads to the 1975 Mr. Universe and Mr. Olympia competitions. The doc normalized bodybuilding, which up to that point had been even more niche than it is today; helped birth the fitness industry; and made a star out of Schwarzenegger, who held the record for most Mr. Olympia wins until Lee Haney won his eighth consecutive title in 1991.

By the '90s, bodybuilding had grown less popular, but the bodies had grown much more impressive. In 1990, WWF mastermind and male-flesh peddler extraordinaire Vince

McMahon launched the World Bodybuilding Federation (WBF), which attempted to merge bodybuilding with the gimmickry of professional wrestling. Things went downhill fast when the following year the WBF instituted a strict steroids testing policy, a result of a roid scandal that roiled the WWF. While pro wrestling is one of the most homoerotic forms of popular entertainment ever, it's the mix of theatricality and physicality that leads to that popularity and transcends the otherwise gay-ass grabbing of crotches, swiveling of hips, hoisting of half-naked men, and glorification of male bodies.

Bodybuilding is just folks standing around posing. It's not terribly interesting to watch, no matter how good a poser a bodybuilder is or how great a body they have. It's not truly accepted as a sport because it's subjective, whereas sports are objective. There are rules, there are points, there is strategy, there is something people can grab onto that holds their attention and rouses their spirits. Bodybuilding will never do that. Therefore, even the "best" bodybuilder in the world, the winner of Mr. Olympia, earns only $400,000. LeBron James makes literally over a hundred times more than that, and he actually puts his body through less trauma.

Though Ferrigno went on to star in *The Incredible Hulk* on television, bodybuilding has never produced another star like Schwarzenegger. Schwarzenegger used bodybuilding to become a star, but most bodybuilders are in it for the passion of it. Muscle is addicting, feeling strong and powerful is addicting, but the long-term effects can be debilitating. Ronnie Coleman, considered along with Schwarzenegger one of the greatest bodybuilders of all time, punished his body with eight-hundred-pound squats and five-hundred-pound bench presses, resulting in several surgeries that left him unable to walk unassisted. Still, he has no regrets save for the bad surgeries. He blames the surgeries for his debilitated condition, and he continues to work out. But at least Coleman made it to the latter half of his life, as opposed to someone like Dallas McCarver, who died of cardiac arrest at twenty-six. There's only one Arnold Schwarzenegger, but there are dozens of bodybuilders whose stories end far more tragically, in violence, in drug abuse, in death. So why do it?

Well, why do anything? Passion. Sure, bodybuilding sometimes makes me feel bad about myself, but so does literally everything. That's the world we live in, one of constantly feeling like shit. But bodybuilding also makes me feel good about myself . . . sometimes . . . most times. Though I may scrutinize every inch of my body, at the end of the day, I love being able to work to realize a childhood dream of who I wanted to be, how I wanted to look. It doesn't make me more of a man, but it does make me feel more myself. And there's the immediacy of it as well.

I can work for years to achieve a goal and never realize it. As a writer, I often feel as if I exist in a void, writing words someone, maybe, is reading somewhere, but I usually never know what those words do to them, how they make them feel, what my impact has been on them, if any. What have I accomplished with those words that will disappear from memory with the next words, or the next show, or movie, or the myriad other distractions pulling at us every moment of every day? With bodybuilding, I know that if I adjust my diet, change my macros, increase my cardio, take my steroids, I will achieve my goal. I can see that achievement in the mirror, week by week, sometimes day by day.

Bodybuilding is the ultimate allegory for how life should be: If you put in the work, you reap the results. But that's not how life works, not always, not often. Life disappoints. Still, the mirror can be a source of affirmation. And with the limited time one has to be a bodybuilder, age and beauty ephemeral as they are, there's also an urgency. Especially for those who don't intend to live into old age, who are determined to get as big as possible, regardless of the costs. That's a version of romantic fatalism that I just can't fuck with—and I love romantic fatalism. Sure, I can understand wholly devoting one's life to an ideal—it's what artists do—but to sacrifice one's life for an ideal is just unnecessary. Art doesn't need to destroy. There should be limits.

I've seen bodybuilders who quit the sport altogether and stop using steroids and advise others never to use them. They look like shrunken versions of themselves but profess to be happy, finally happy. There seems to be a lot of misery in bodybuilding, a lot of mental health issues that often go undiscussed because of the sport's culture. Suffering is part of the game. Suffer and don't bitch; don't be a pussy. No pain, no gain.

I've noticed that attitude slowly changing as bodybuilders and fitness professionals take to Instagram to open up about their struggles with depression, suicidal ideation, and drug use—and steroid use has been linked to further substance abuse. It's heartening to see all these gym bros getting in touch with their feelings.

But at the same time, it's been heartbreaking to see others in the bodybuilding community targeting trans people, as seems to be the modus operandi of the conservative movement in America, to which bodybuilders tend to overwhelmingly belong.

You'd think the bodybuilding community would realize they have some things in common with the trans community, as everyone involved wants to manifest their ideal body. Often with the implementation of hormones. Yet bodybuilders, particularly those in America, where steroids are illegal, have been begrudging of and mocking toward trans people, and trans youth, for their access to testosterone, the baseline steroid for gym bros universal.

Part of this is the general animus conservative America holds against the trans community, which anyone not deafened by a right-wing echo chamber knows is just a distraction technique by conservatives to avoid actually taking care of their constituents. Instead, trans people are a threat to our children, they're a threat to the social order, they're an affront to god and nature, etc., etc. These sentiments trickle down into the bodybuilding community, where loves of steroids and guns go hand in hand and masculinity reaches peak toxicity. I can't tell you how many times I've been following a bodybuilder on Instagram, scrolling through his posts, chasing a boner, and I run into an AK-47 or claims of the 2020 election being stolen. Boner sufficiently killed.

As much as I love bodybuilding, I can't ever feel a part of its community because of these vestiges of homophobia, transphobia, and conservatism. There are plenty of gay men who willingly buy into, or simply ignore, these tenets to satiate that all-consuming hunger for muscle, one that, like mine, probably gestated in their youth. That hunger can be maddening; it can be delirious, rhapsodic, even. These muscle kweens might feel, as I often do, that they have more in common with the bodybuilding community than the gay community.

But, again, I also find commonality between the bodybuilding community and the gay community, not to mention a symbiosis. Hell, AIDS patients used to supply bodybuilders with human growth hormone because HGH helped mitigate the wasting effects of the disease. With that kind of history—as well as the history of financial support and sustained enthusiasm for the sport amid waning desire from everyone else—you'd think bodybuilders would be more considerate of the queer community, but you could say the same for America at large. Of all the things minority groups have given to America—the economy that dominates the world, the culture that seduces it—some would prefer to focus on what minorities have taken or changed or somehow denied them.

Bodybuilders are often stereotyped as meatheads or bullies, stereotypes that persist because they're kind of true. Picking on trans kids, who are still kids, because they get legal testosterone is the epitome of being a bully—targeting, regardless of one's feelings about the trans community, the most vulnerable people in our society. Blindly following along with rhetoric instead of actively questioning it is meathead behavior.

And yet, there's so much knowledge involved in being a bodybuilder, stuff I'm still struggling to wrap my head around.

It's a shame, really, that bodybuilding gets such a bad rap when there are so many positive stories that come from it as well.

On social media, those who have struggled with their mental health often reveal that when they were at their lowest, bodybuilding was the only constant in their lives, and by staying committed to it, they managed to turn their lives around and, in turn, inspire others. I hate inspiring others, but bodybuilding has definitely been a life raft for me in the choppiest of waters. It's helped pull me out of funks, it's given me a better sense of self, it's gotten me laid a lot. The steroid use and the muscle dysmorphia are, to me, just a part of the deal. Not everyone will understand or agree with that, but it's not for everyone. It's for me. And it's no one else's business, really.

Autonomy over one's body, after all, should be a sacred right. Whether that means transitioning or terminating a pregnancy or sticking some testosterone in your ass cheeks three times a week. And the government should make it easier, and thus safer, to do those things, instead of making it harder, further endangering people's lives. And if that's not a compelling enough argument, one could always hit Uncle Sam with that tried and true rebuttal, "You're not our fucking dad!" Works every time.

3

NIGGER LOVER

"**DO YOU MIND** if I call you the N-word?" (*pant, pant*)

"Um . . . ?" (*pant*)

"It's just what I'm into. It's okay if not." (*pant, pant*)

"Yeah, no." (*pant*)

"Cool." (*pant*) "Put it in my ass." (*pant, pant*)

That was a real exchange I had with an otherwise lovely young white gentleman one summer afternoon in Provincetown, I wanna say in 2018. His casualness in asking me was the real shocker, not the asking itself. He was so matter-of-fact about it. He went on to say that he loved Black guys and he wasn't racist, but something about getting fucked by a Black guy and calling him "nigger" (he never actually said the word around me) really got his mojo working. He didn't know why.

I did. I just didn't feel like unpacking it with him, not when I was already balls-deep, after having been so horny all week. This hunky white boy had said he'd seen me at the pool earlier and that I had piqued his interest as I was reading amid all the loud pool noises and the blaring electronica soundtrack. I felt greatly flattered. Boys into books are just generally hotter than other boys. He was so nice and so handsome and so sculpted and fine.

And then he had to go and say something like that. Who says romance is dead?

SO THIS GUY, he lived in Boston; he even went to Vassar, a most liberal of liberal arts colleges, in my hometown of Poughkeepsie. He was your classic Democratic homosexual, probably posting black squares and "Black Lives Matter" hashtags during the summer of 2020. At least he wasn't the type of shitty hypocritical white gay who has #BLM in his Grindr profile yet still can't bring himself to acknowledge my fucking existence. But he's the kind of fag who doesn't think he harbors any sort of racial animus; in fact, he loves Black boys, so he can't possibly be racist. Therefore, he doesn't really mean anything if and when he says "nigger," since it's not like he's cosigning the meaning behind it.

It's like when little white boys rap along to their favorite lyrics and "forget" to omit the N-bombs. They love Black culture, even if they're being dismissive of Black people. It's one thing to be rejected or ignored for your Black skin; it's another to be prized for it. Both make me uncomfortable, but I suppose it's better to be desired than not. Still, it's altogether terrible to be reduced to one aspect of yourself, an aspect over which you have no control. Every individual contains multitudes.

What this Beantown himbo didn't understand is that at this point in American history, racism is like the air we breathe—inhaled and exhaled without a second thought. What he got off on wasn't the word but the power dynamic that word represents. Even if I'm on top, he can reclaim dominance by putting me in my place, the way white people have been using "nigger" for centuries.

The following year, 2019, I was in Miami, as part of a cross-country journey moving from New York to Los Angeles. New York and Miami are like sister cities, connected by convenient, short, cheap flights, so that some New Yorkers and Miami . . . ites(?) regularly migrate from one city to the other. One of these bi-city residents messaged me on Grindr, and while I found him attractive, I didn't feel like hooking up with him. He was an older, white muscle-daddy type, which is very much *my* type, but for whatever reason, I wasn't into him. Attraction is capricious, and I go through different cravings—sometimes younger, sometimes older, bigger or smaller, open to any race but with a fondness for white boys. He wasn't my flavor that day. I usually just ignore messages, hoping that guys will get the hint. As much as I hate getting rejected, I hate rejecting guys even more. I know how it feels, and I don't want to subject someone else to that. But someone's feelings, or pride, get hurt regardless of intention.

This daddy kept messaging me, so I decided to be a big boy and just say that I wasn't interested. Hopefully he would be understanding about it. Or, you know, not. When I told him politely that I wasn't interested, he responded curtly, "Fuck you. Nigger." Then after he had made sure he had given me enough time to read his missive, he blocked me. I swear, the ability to block people has been one of the primary causes of the breakdown of civilized society. Folks are out here just saying the wildest shit without consequences because they can simply block whomever they offend. And we can curate who is privy to our lives and thoughts and opinions, eradicating anyone who might disagree.

That and it's just fucking rude. To say that to me and just disappear into the ether was such a pussy-ass move, and it left me feeling conflicted. On the one hand I was angry. Like, just because I said no, in as diplomatic a way as possible, I'm a nigger? I was also partly amused that someone could get so butt-hurt when he had so much going for him. As I mentioned, he was an attractive dude; lived between New York and Miami, so he had money; and had a nice body. I'm sure he was used to getting what he wanted. But that entitlement didn't extend to my body. And the more I thought about it, the sadder and angrier I became. In the year of our Lord Oprah, 2019, I'm out in these streets getting called the N-word? Did Obama mean nothing?!

Of course not. I was more surprised when Barack Obama won in 2008 than I was when Donald Trump won in 2016. The latter felt correct. The balance restored. The former seemed a fluke. Obama was a once-in-a-generation president who thankfully was Black. Trump was a run-of-the-mill charlatan who of course was white. But with Obama's presidency, the nation—parts of it, anyway—was eager to continue the fluke, thinking this was the way things were now. The straight white man's reign of terror had finally come to an end.

Yeah, right. Americans underestimated the power of whiteness—even white people are afraid of it. If you don't have whiteness then you're just a nigger, the antithesis of whiteness, and no one wants to be a nigger. White people so feared their own niggerization, the loss of their power, they nearly drove this country right into the ditch.

For this entitled white man to brand me a nigger then block me with impunity was his show of power. He reclaimed it. I was put in my place. Balance was restored.

Just as people (let's be clear: certain white people) thought Obama was a radical and permanent sea change, so it went the summer of the Great Reckoning. The lynching of George Floyd was the spark, but dozens of other instances of police brutality against people of color were the kindling. White America had a nice long look in the mirror and didn't like what it saw. After all, we were in the middle of a pandemic, so it wasn't like anyone had anything better to do. The whites started reading anti-racist literature, attended Black Lives Matter protests in droves, and asked their Black friends what to do, how to feel, and just if they were okay.

I don't know a Black person who wasn't *exhausted* that summer. Between the pandemic, the violence, the rampant injustice, the marching, and the white guilt. And I'm not even an activist. I've never taken on that label because I'm just too lazy and self-involved. I'm not one to march anywhere. I might hold a sign if I don't have to go anywhere or have to stand for long periods of time. I'm not even an armchair activist, sharing posts to show how socially conscious I am. While I was moved by the deaths of George Floyd, and Breonna Taylor, and

Ahmaud Arbery, and the list goes on and on and on, I had also become inured to this violence, to this injustice. It wasn't that I didn't care. How could I not? I just can't bring myself to watch any video depicting a police officer assaulting an unarmed Black person, because it's too easy to imagine that person being me.

GETTING INCARCERATED IS almost a rite of passage for Black men. It's expected of us. And though I've spent my life consciously defying, or trying to defy, expectations, I still found myself in jail. Just once, though. I say "just" because I probably skated by a few more times than I should have, given how often I was blackout drunk in the streets of New York City. Sniffing cocaine in every alleyway and bathroom in that town, face-planting off a mysterious combination of pills, and carried *Weekend at Bernie's* style all around the city; phones and wallets were lost with careless, drunken abandon. That I only ended up in jail once is kind of a minor miracle. My own recklessness, combined with the likelihood of me, a Black man, ending up in jail or prison, and it seems more miraculous the older I get.

I used to think that because I defied expectations I was exceptional. That I would never be a nigger, when I understood a nigger to be a lowly Black person. I looked down on the variation "nigga," and down on niggas who used it as "nigger." Only later did I realize this was a form of self-loathing around my own Blackness. I had to embrace the nigga in me.

As with any and every story leading to my downfall, this one begins with my being horny. I get *dangerously* horny. It's the Scorpio in me. Though I may write a big game, I don't sleep around a lot. Sex with strangers, pretty much like doing anything with strangers, is awkward and potentially dangerous, so I've always sought some sort of consistency with my sexual partners, even if they don't do the same. But all that "patiently waiting" business weighs heavy on a body, and my balls, and after months of denying myself some man-lovin', I erupt into a cipher of longing. I need to get laid, no matter the cost.

During one of these particular horned-up jags, I was on antibiotics after contracting an infection from the removal of one of my remaining wisdom teeth. Because I was an asshole (still am, honestly), I was out drinking on these antibiotics, then someone brought out the cocaine, and next thing I knew I was knocking on the door of an old hookup. I was apparently a bit worse for wear and was asked to leave several minutes into the action. I was so furious as I gathered my things and stormed out the door, sternly telling him to lose my number. It was late by then, around three in the morning. The trains wouldn't have been running so much as crawling, but I began walking toward the subway station anyway. Hopefully my luck would hold out tonight. Or, you know, not.

As I walked, I worked myself into a real heated lather, angry that yet again I was denied what I wanted, the simplest of pleasures. Never mind it was my fault, as wasted as I was, but I thought I was fine. I think I went to the train, but it wouldn't be arriving for quite some time, so I went to sit in front of a store instead of waiting on the platform. I kept talking to myself, making myself angrier and angrier, the rage burning inside me until I slapped my hand on the window of the store.

I don't know what I thought would happen. I certainly didn't think the entire window would shatter and an alarm would go off. Or that my hand would start bleeding. I knew I had to get out of there, so I tried to hail a cab. Hailing a cab as a Black man, with the nerve to go to Brooklyn from Manhattan at three in the morning, was already a gamble, but my bloodied hand truly did me in. The cabbie called the cops, who put together the ringing alarm and broken glass and handcuffed me in an ambulance on the way to the hospital, to get stitches in my hand, and then to jail. To wait.

Jail, by the way, is no fun. I had grown up thinking jail was like that episode of *The Golden Girls* when Dorothy, Blanche, and Rose get mistaken for sex workers (yeah, okay) and land in the clink—just as they had gotten tickets to see Mr. Burt Reynolds! That jail was full of hijinks. Rose met a hooker from St. Olaf and convinced her to go back home and give up her life of sin, and Dorothy, naturally, became the alpha dog. Then when Sophia comes to bail them out of jail, she thinks that means one of the jailbirds will be staying home so she can go see Mr. Burt Reynolds, too. When the girls inform her that no, she'll still be sitting this one out, Sophia runs off with all the tickets, leaving them in jail. Fun!

I didn't make any friends in jail. The closest I came was with this hustler who, as soon as he got into the cell, faked a seizure and tried to get me to play along. It was just him and me in the cell, but he feigned paralysis, which I limply cosigned. I was then moved to a crowded cell with other men, mostly Black and brown, mostly drunk. There was one toilet that we were expected to use in front of everybody. I held in all I could and tried to get some sleep on the concrete blocks the NYPD calls beds.

But I couldn't sleep. I just kept thinking about how the hell this had happened. *Why* the hell this had happened. Dangerously horny. Damn this Scorpio energy! At first I was angry at my hookup for rejecting me, sending me on this downward spiral, but soon that anger turned to disappointment in myself. This had all started because I was being an asshole and decided to drink and do coke on antibiotics because that was how I operated in my twenties. Anything for a good time, anything to keep the sadness at bay. But I was nearing thirty and I didn't want to be that person anymore. That mess. The passed-out kid in the corner. The lifeless, bloodied body on the sidewalk. Sure, those incidents make for funny anecdotes that I will tell till the day I die. But we have such a small window to be reckless with our lives—and being a Black man meant I couldn't really afford to be reckless in the first place if I was to achieve all that I wanted in this grand, beautiful, painful, glorious existence— and I had smashed that window to pieces.

I was so lucky until I wasn't. I made it out of Poughkeepsie, I went to NYU, and even after I dropped out, I managed to become a professional writer. I defied the odds until I could no longer. My mistakes, my messiness, caught up with me. I got out of jail the following evening, the sun setting over lower Manhattan. It was late 2015; I would turn thirty that November. I had to be more careful.

My arresting officer was this very nice Black girl with great braids, and she handled me gently, speaking to me in a calm, reassuring tone and asking me if the cuffs were too tight. I could've been her brother or her cousin. With the cuffs on, I had sobered up quickly and was coherent and adamant that this was all just one big accident. The store, it turns out, had insurance, and that paid for the window. I appeared in court, paid a fine to the city, and the felony was expunged from my record. Again, lucky as *fuck*. I knew it was luck and that this was a wake-up call. The alternative was frightening.

I was born in Guyana, where my citizenship lies, and I am still, as of this writing but hopefully not for much longer, just a permanent resident of America. If I got into enough trouble, I could potentially get kicked out of the country. I've been here since I was four years old. I have no life in Guyana. The reasons why I haven't gotten my citizenship are numerous and complicated, but losing my life was not always my biggest fear should I have a run-in with the law. Then the summer of 2020 happened and I was reminded that maybe it should be.

Because of the immediacy of the George Floyd killing—because "it could've been me"—I felt I should want to do more, to get out into the streets, march, yell, hold signs while *moving*. I should demonstrably care more. Was I a bad Black person for not marching? I've often felt like a bad Black person, whether it was my "fondness" for white boys, or never feeling like I fit in with other Black people, or being embarrassed by niggers, what Black people call other Black people they can't stand. "Nigga" is a term of endearment or humor or anything you want it to be, similar to how I use and feel about "faggot." Because I am both of these things, I feel like I can choose what they mean and how to use them since, historically, I, and people like me, didn't have that choice. But once we, Black folk, add the "-er," somebody done ruined everything for everybody.

So-called respectable Blacks might not even use "nigga" because they feel it diminishes the race, but if some ignorant coon comes shuffling along, they'll whip out that "-er" with the quickness. It's not a form of racism when Black people use the hard N-word on one another; it's more about class. One person's got it; the other does not. But no matter: whosoever wields "nigger" in anger, or passion, or frivolity, or any fucking situation, does so as an act of ignominy. While I couldn't possibly consider myself respectable, just based on the last few pages alone, I've often said under my breath to Black folks disgracing the race, "Fucking niggers." Or, "I hate niggers." In one breath I can love Black people and hate niggers. But then, it took me a while to love being Black.

'CAUSE I USED to want to be white. I thought life would be easier, that I would be more desirable, and of course that's true, but I had to realize that it was my Blackness, like my queerness, that made me exceptional, not the denial or transcendence of them. I had to understand the history of the African American and the impossibly impossible odds they surmounted to become the most influential people in the world. I had to learn to find myself—and by extension all Black people—beautiful. Some Black folks are born feeling those things, the love and pride of being Black. I don't know why I wasn't.

When I was young, being Black felt like a burden I had been

saddled with, made even worse by being a big old kween. Other Black kids made fun of me, told me I sounded white or was trying to be white because I was a nerd who actually liked school. And as I got older, I was put in more and more gifted classes, which grew less and less Black year over year.

Still, my mother enrolled me in a free after-school program that also had a summer camp, not the sleepaway kind, but the day kind, where a van came to pick us up one by one and dropped us off at some abandoned school in the City of Poughkeepsie. It was called Harambee, Swahili for "all put together" and the motto of Kenya. Harambee was intended for low-income, mostly Black kids whose parents needed somewhere to send them where they would be fed and, god willing, kept out of trouble. For my single mother, who was almost forty-two when she had me and thus had no energy for my shenanigans, Harambee and programs like it were incredibly important. For me, Harambee was a scary experience that I eventually grew to enjoy. The scariest place for a chubby, effeminate, soft-spoken gay kid is the school bus. The Poughkeepsie City School District didn't provide buses; the closest we got were discounted fares for the city buses, which were especially dangerous because those kids loved to get rowdy in the morning. Harambee had vans, which were as terrifying as buses, maybe more so because they were so small—much easier to grab, hit, and throw things. And the driver was not what one would call "giving a damn."

So at the start of Harambee's summer program, I timidly stepped onto the van and kept to myself. I was a sly one. Everyone thought I was so quiet and shy, but that was only one side of me. The safe side. But Harambee allowed me to come out of my shell just enough. One year, each class (we were divided into classes) had to perform in the big end-of-summer show. Nothing brings out the ham in me like the threat and thrill of showtime. I loved to sing and dance but kept those parts of myself hidden from nearly everyone else. Still, when the time came, I grabbed my chance to shine with both hands and shook it vigorously in excitement.

I worked hard during rehearsals, sweating so profusely that our counselor, a cute, obsidian-skinned high school student who was about fourteen, pointed me out as an example of how hard everyone else should be working. Cue the side-eyes and sucked teeth. But we pulled our dance together, performing for our parents, who dutifully applauded. Harambee taught me about Kwanzaa, and I was so intrigued by the idea that I insisted to my mother that we should celebrate it. We didn't, but give a kid some credit for trying. Because I still remember the song our counselors taught us—"Fanga alafia, ashe, ashe," a West African welcome song of peace—Harambee was probably the first time I had been taught Black pride. It was a lesson, however, that took years to fully sink in.

I was wishing I was white as late as my sophomore year at college, when I lamented as much to my co-workers at my work-study job at NYU's payroll office, to their great shock. I gathered that was not something one said out loud.

Like my queerness, I had to come into my Blackness on my own terms and in my own time. Throughout my school years, I was lucky enough to have a few Black women teachers who each left an indelible mark on me. There was my fifth-grade teacher, Ms. Howard, who took me to Boston at the end of the school year as a sort of prize for being her top student. Ms. Jackson, my ninth-grade English teacher, taught us Jamaica Kincaid's *Annie John*, a novel that spoke to my own West Indian roots. And my twelfth-grade English teacher, Ms. Ricketts, spent months that I cherished teaching us Toni Morrison's epic *Song of Solomon* and also helped me write my college essay.

As I did with my queer coming-of-age, I attempted to immerse myself in Black literature. I've never seen *Roots*, but I read it. And Alex Haley's other seminal work, *The Autobiography of Malcolm X*. I fell in love with James Baldwin, as every gay Black boy should. I fell in love with Toni Morrison's *Beloved*, as every human being should. I didn't go as deep as I did with the queer canon, however. Though the books I did read offered me an insight into love, and that was what I craved most of all. But diving, no matter how shallow the plunge, through Black literature and history did help awaken me to the joys of being Black, though I think hip-hop played an even bigger part.

I grew up during one of the last true golden ages of our time, the golden age of '90s hip-hop and R&B. When hits—bangers! bops! classics galore!—were being shat out by every diva, boy group, girl group, rap group, and spotlight-hogging producer around. I was besotted with the R&B side of things, rap being a bit too hard for my young ears. But by the time I got to high school, the '90s were coming to an end and we were entering the glorious age of pop-rap, when rap crossed over so hard, displacing rock as the predominant music genre in America. With the deaths of Tupac and Biggie, rap got less confrontational (but not completely) and more radio friendly. We had hooks, kids. Knockout collabos.

Rap and its prodigious use of "faggot" in the most derogatory way had alienated me when I was a kid, but as a teenager with a questionably booming social life, the rap-R&B songs of the early aughts provided my daily soundtrack. I grew to love rap, and as I do with everything I love, I completely immersed myself in it. I went back to the '90s and listened, really listened, to the best that decade had to offer. Nas's *Illmatic* was pure poetry, the Fugees' *The Score* was epic, and Biggie's *Ready to Die* was terrifying, vigorous, and flawless. Missy Elliott's *Supa Dupa Fly* was and still is the future.

I grew to love the art of hip-hop—the richness in its storytelling, the wit in its rhymes, the audaciousness of its Blackness—and I admired its global takeover, how rap crossed oceans and cultures. I remember an article in *Vibe* magazine, one of my favorite reads, about how kids in Japan, always ahead of a trend, were dyeing their skin brown to be more like African Americans, wearing FUBU and all that. *How weird*, I thought. *Blackface is back!* And then I started to piece it all together. How deep the influence of Black people went, how we turned tragedy into triumph, how "nigga" was such a great fucking word that could be used in nearly any context, like "you" or "the." It took me a while, but I grew to love, honor, respect, and protect my Blackness. And I also realized there was no "correct" way to be Black.

Yes, there are some experiences that are universal to us, but Black people come in all shades, varieties, variants, and varietals. Most of us, save for some very prominent exceptions, wish Black people as a community the best, because when Black people win, everyone wins. In a fair and just society, no one is a nigger.

AS I WAS growing prouder in my Blackness, I was also confronted with the ways Blackness was perceived and treated within the gay community. So much of what we consider gay culture is Black queer culture—the same can be said about American culture in general. Scrolling through Instagram, I'm always amused and slightly horrified by all these straight, white, middle-aged folk yapping like a gaggle of Black kweens outside the beauty supply. Everyone's working and slaying and voguing and popping whatever ass they think they have. And this extends to more than just vernacular; it's fashion, it's hair, it's attitude, it's a whole-ass appropriation. But nowhere have I witnessed more blatantly a love of Black culture but a dismissal of Black people than among the gays.

Until about a decade ago, the names Marsha P. Johnson and Sylvia Rivera were all but lost to history, except for the tireless activists who kept their names and legacies alive. With the increased visibility of trans people came the increased awareness of trans history, including Marsha's and Sylvia's pivotal roles in the Stonewall uprising and the birth of the modern gay rights movement. With gays finally finding a voice, cis white men took on the most visible leadership roles in the movement, leaving trans and gender-nonconforming folks out in the cold. Until they got tired of being relegated to the back seat. The victory of same-sex marriage, passed under the first Black president, felt like the beginning of a radical progression in American society, not a culmination, which is what it was.

Activists had been working for decades to be recognized as full citizens, with the Black civil rights movement inspiring the tactics of the LGBTQ+ civil rights movement. The gays and the Black Panthers even worked together at one point. The Panthers also reached across the aisle to the labor movement, which was why they had to be destroyed. As soon as the downtrodden realize they're all fighting a common enemy, that enemy's days are numbered. White gays, however, don't always see themselves as the downtrodden, not when they're still white men and thus still profit from the maintenance of a system created by and for white men. Once those faggots got gay marriage, their struggle was over.

On August 15, 1970, in New York City, Black Panther Party co-founder and future destroyed Black Panther Huey Newton delivered a speech in full-voiced support of the women's and gay liberation movements. He urged "respect and feelings for all oppressed people," stating his belief that homosexuals "might be the most oppressed people in the society." And being the most oppressed, they could potentially "be the most revolutionary." Newton emphasized that the oppressed all have the same oppressor—not necessarily the White Man, as he conceded that the poorest white person is "the most racist because he is afraid that he might lose something."

Newton's vision was of a coalition of the oppressed throwing off the shackles of oppression, and it behooved Black people to find commonality with others in a similar position. In that speech, which feels radical even today, Newton contradicted the age-old myth that Black people are somehow more homophobic than white people, when homophobia is one of the few things all races can agree on. It's magical that way. While so much is made of Black people being homophobic, what of gays being racist?

GRINDR LAUNCHED IN 2009, in the early days of the apps, and I was taken aback by the hostility from some white men and taken further aback by the naked, disrespectful lust from some others. It's one thing to be told "No Blacks" by a headless white torso in response to something as admittedly forward as "Hi," but it's another to be propositioned for some reverse slave-play action by a white man who insists on your racial superiority. Is a goddamn "Hello, how are you?" too much to ask for?

The apps feel like the last place in American society where it's okay to be blatantly racist. Everywhere else there's at least some subtlety. Things have gotten better than when I first started out on them, I will say that. After being called out by other gays, from their fellow white gays to gay journalists (myself included), white gays at least stopped, for the most part, putting things like "No Blacks, no fats, no Asians, no femmes" in their profiles. They found less offensive, more subtle ways to express their racial preference. One guy had something like, "I like guys that look like me." That same guy came up to me after I had moderated a panel discussing gay dating apps, including the racist bias on them, and was surprisingly "hey gurl"–level chummy. I had messaged him on the apps previously, but he had ignored me then. I wasn't suitable for a sexual or romantic partner, but we could kiki like gal pals.

I don't think most white gays see their sexual racism as racism at all. For years, they dismissed it as simply their "preference." But I liked to point out, repeatedly and in print, that favoring one race over another isn't a preference; it's actually the textbook definition of racism. "But we're all attracted to who we're attracted to," they argued, and I agree. I wish I wasn't attracted to white boys at all, but here we are. The difference is I don't discount other races altogether. I can find anyone of any race attractive, but the weakness I have for white boys isn't a preference. It's a weakness. It's programming. It's a reflection of the racial hierarchy of America.

For some white men, my Blackness has a sheen of sexual attraction, as well as the preexisting cool. They want me because I'm Black. How flattering for me. These white gays definitely don't see themselves as racist. They love Black guys! As they will tell you before even giving their names. They love big Black cock! BBC4LIFE! I'm never not offended by that kind of rhetoric. Because, for one, these guys are almost never hot. Having struck out with the more attractive members of their own race, some white guys find Black boys easy (or at least easier) pickings. That in it itself is an insult, as if I'm supposed to settle for less and be grateful for the attention of *any* white man. And the ones who are hot become less so once they say something along the lines of "Mmm, chocolate." Bon appétit, motherfuckers.

The affront to my shallowness notwithstanding, I also don't

want to be reduced to my race when I contain multitudes, just as I don't like those multitudes dismissed by virtue of my race. It's reductive either way. Though admittedly it hurts considerably less to be coveted than dismissed. For a Black boy routinely dismissed by white men, finding a worshipful white man, regardless of their attraction to that white man, feels like a respite from the pain of rejection.

How can I put this delicately? You know what, fuck it, I'm not going to: I've noticed a lot of really hot Black guys with really mediocre white men. I'm particularly sensitive to noticing these pairings because I see myself among those really hot Black guys—and sometimes, I actually have been. I wonder if they were just seduced by their partner's whiteness or by being treated like some Black king, or at the very least, treated with respect, when so many other white men hadn't. And regardless, are they happy? Or does it not matter since they're not alone?

I CAN'T REALLY interrogate the white gaze of white gays without interrogating my own Black gaze of Black gays. Jack'd launched in 2010, a year after Grindr. The very whiteness and racism running rampant on Grindr birthed this other app, which caters to people of color. Because it's expressly for people of color, users, myself included, don't have to worry as much about the micro- and macroaggressions on the more popular Grindr and Scruff, also founded in 2010.

I use all three apps, but Jack'd is more of a last resort when I'm not pulling peen on the other two. If I'm being ignored by a bunch of white guys or being buzzed about by the chococrazed, I can turn to Jack'd, which promotes itself as "an app for all of us," as if tacitly acknowledging the fact that Grindr and Scruff are not for "us." Meanwhile, the same company that owns Scruff also owns Jack'd.

Sure, I can rely on Jack'd to give me a boost in attention, if not necessarily self-esteem, but I also look down on the kind of guys who use Jack'd. Niggers. The "down-low" "homothugs" who can't string together a simple sentence, who don't have photos, or who use a photo of a city backdrop or a placid lake in place of their face. Though Black people may not be more homophobic than white people, Black queer men still don't feel comfortable being out in their communities because they might not feel safe or respected if they are. Or they just don't want anyone in their business. Whatever it may be, Jack'd and Grindr have the same amount of DL, picless, discreet profiles; it's just that the ones on Jack'd are all Black.

As a bougie Black faggot, I naturally look down on these other faggots. I grew up around thugs, and I don't find them attractive. I used to fear them, walking quickly past them on Main Street on my way home, my head down, avoiding eye contact, deaf to anything they might try to say to me. The homothugs—the use of which makes me feel like a middle-aged white daytime talk show host from the late '90s, when "homothugs" were treated as a phenomenon—I encounter on Jack'd just remind me of that fear. Having some college under my belt, and having been accused of speaking like I was white since I was a kid, I feel like I have less in common with some DL Black boy from the block than some nerdy white boy from Connecticut.

It's interesting how our desires can reveal who we really are. A liberal white boy may wholeheartedly believe in and support Black Lives Matter but only date, and may only be friends with, guys who look like him. Does that make him racist? Kinda. Racism isn't always intentional, and race, and the feelings we're taught to have about race, influence nearly every interaction we have as human beings, whether or not we acknowledge or are aware of it. Counteracting racism has to be a deliberate action. But you also have to care enough and want to be anti-racist for your actions to make sense. Otherwise, it's fine to not do anything if you don't believe in it. It's actually preferable for everyone involved.

I may denounce racism and classism, but at the end of the day, I'm just another respectable Black, thumbing my nose at those I deem niggers. Am I classist? Totally. I may have grown up poor, but I also grew up with an unearned sense of entitlement. Sure, I may hate capitalism, but I also like nice things. I contain multitudes. And that's not always a great thing.

Class is a deeper problem in America because class begat race. There had to be a class system for Black people to be second-class citizens . . . once we were actually granted citizenship. Before that, we weren't even considered people, or at least not more than three-fifths of one. A class of human beings stripped of their humanity by virtue of their skin color.

Within class there are racial hierarchies, and within race are class hierarchies. Hence, niggers. The lowest of the low. I would never date a nigger. My own class prejudices won't allow it. And my own levels of oppression don't soften or alter my stance.

It's interesting how our desires can reveal who we really are—"Do you mind if I call you the N-word?"

AS MUCH AS white boys have a reductive view of me, I have a reductive view of other Black gays. There's a palpable tension whenever one only Black kween encounters another only Black kween. In a sea of whiteness and/or heterosexuality, we can either be the best of friends or the worst of enemies. There's a wariness that very much says, "I see you. Bitch." This other Black kween could threaten the place of the one and only Black kween, or they might blow up everything that the one and only kween has worked to cultivate. They're family, but they could be friend or foe.

When I first started working at a fashion blog, there was another, younger Black kween named Mac already working there. I thought I might have to kill him. Highlander "THERE CAN BE ONLY ONE!" style. If there was already a Black kween there, what would they do with me? Wasn't the quota filled? It's so hard and rare to get an opportunity that when someone else who looks like you also gets that opportunity, you feel less special and thus threatened. But Mac ended up becoming one of my dearest friends. Which is usually how those standoffs go. We as minorities—double minorities at that—tend to underestimate the power of having another person we don't have to explain everything to.

The Tenth is a magazine founded around 2015 by Khary Septh, André Jones, and Kyle Banks, three Black queer creatives with the intention of turning a side-eye to queer white media. Theirs was a highly cultivated side-eye for art and fashion on a level I hadn't associated with Black queerness before. As a consumer, I always want anything Black to be luxurious, because we deserve luxury. Not just luxury in terms of cars and jewels and what have you, but the luxury of quality, beautiful photography, provocative art, spell-checked and grammatically correct prose. When Black products fall short of these goals, it's disappointing but not totally surprising. After all, it was probably made for a quarter of what its white counterpart was, by people who might not have the same wherewithal or opportunities as their white creative counterparts. *The Tenth* wanted to change that. They wanted to bring luxury to the gurls!

I first read about them in *The New York Times* (fancy bitches) and reached out to them for an interview for my then outlet, *Queerty*, a small, independent, white-owned queer news and pop culture site. I met up with Khary and Kyle in Brooklyn, near their studio, and we chatted for hours. They were so fucking cool and smart. Khary had worked for years in fashion as a creative director, and Kyle was, among other things, an opera singer. These were the faggots I wanted to know. We kept in touch, and I would write for *The Tenth* here and there over the years. I hung out with Khary, Kyle, and a few of their collaborators on their recent issue about a year or so after our first meeting.

We were just kiki'ing in their studio loft space, drinking, getting high, yelling about Whitney and Janet, and it felt like we were changing the world. We creatives, with so much in common, whom I could talk to as if I had known them my whole life, as if we had been raised together, even though I barely knew any of them. I felt so fucking Black, so fucking queer, so fucking powerful. For years I had been chasing whiteness, but among these gorgeous Black kweens I found what I had been really searching for: affirmation. I felt part of something. And it emboldened me to further embrace my Blackness.

The Tenth was trying to change the perception of Black queerness in the media, but with the understanding that in order to change others' perceptions, we had to change our perception of ourselves. We had to believe that we *deserved*. That we deserved luxury, that we deserved the same resources, the same opportunities. We had to stop seeking permission from the white gaze. And the white gays. We had to believe that *we* weren't what *they* said we were: niggers. We had to stop seeing one another as niggers and start seeing one another as "my niggas." It's a tall order, but Black folks have been chipping away at that hard "-er" for centuries.

4

MEMOIR OF A BLOUSE

YOU KNOW THOSE moments when you just feel *seen?* When the universe gives you a little chuck under the chin, like, "Hey, kiddo . . ." It's the small things. It's when you're bored at a party and don't know anyone or want to know anyone, but then someone casually drops a quote from any *Real Housewives* franchise. It's when you're one of two fags at the supermarket and ". . . Baby One More Time" comes on and you both shimmy-and-a-dip at the correct part of the song. It's when you're one of two Black people literally anywhere, and though you never say a word, some white person does something white and you two just catch each other's eyes and shake your heads.

I was listening to the *Las Culturistas* podcast, hosted by comedians and noted homosexuals Bowen Yang and Matt Rogers, and they have the kind of synergistic repartee I have with my gay friends. The gals can banter. And during one such banter session, Bowen had said something that resonated to Matt's very core, and Matt said, with such endearing earnestness, "We are *such . . . sisters*." He went on to try to explain what he meant, that they had a kindred bond that felt not like a sweaty, smelly brotherhood but like a deep and loving sisterhood. But we all knew what she meant. I see you. And in the words of Kandi Burruss, "We see each *otha*."

I call my gays my sisters all the time. At some point, I started invoking the Rosemary Clooney–Vera-Ellen "Sisters" number from *White Christmas*—because I am very much *that* gay—and started sing-calling them my *sistersssssss. Sistersssssss*. Nothing can come between sistersssss! When a certain gentleman came from Rome, guess what? We both fucked him. Because that's what gay sisters do. Let the straights have their bros; we got our sisses. I have a brother, and I can tell you firsthand, brotherhood ain't shit. But the sisterhood I have with my gays is special, sacred. We are family. I got all my *sistersssssss* with me.

I hate it when someone tries to herd all of us together and refers to us as "boys." "Come on, boys!" That feels needlessly aggressive. This isn't softball. Me and my gays are the girls. Or gurls. Ladies, if you're feeling generous. I refer to myself as "she" or "her" all the time. Both playfully and earnestly. Gay men have been doing that for ages. It was our way of reclaiming the joke, the joke being us and how effeminate we, gay men, are. The sissies. The queens. The faggots. All used derogatively and all reclaimed by us sisses, kweens, and fags.

I thought to be gay was to straddle the gender divide playfully. Tap dancing on a tightrope between male and female. He could be she; she could be me. But it was all just a form of play.

And I was so happy to play! When I was a baby gay, I couldn't be a sissy. As an adult gay, it was freeing to be as faggy as I wanted to be.

So masculinity wasn't something that I actually took seriously. When I started dating, or started trying to date, it came as a surprise to me just how seriously other kweens took it.

FOR SOME REASON, I thought gay men would be beyond the whole "masculinity" thing because, well, taking a dick is perhaps the most effeminate thing a man could realistically do. It's not like we can give birth, but being penetrated is fulfilling the most traditional of female roles: receptacle. But I've never successfully bottomed, so I can't tell you what it feels like. Not for lack of trying, by the way. When I first attempted to have sex, I assumed I would be a bottom because . . . she is me. I am she. Sissies aren't tops. But penetrating me was like trying to get into Fort Knox—it involved tools, methods, and skills very few men possess. So I became a top out of necessity. I always told myself, and anyone who'd listen, that I'd one day be vers, just as soon as I found someone I was comfortable enough with to pop my proverbial cherry. Nearly two decades later, here I am. Still unpopped.

I do know that being a top does make me *feel* more manly. I could assemble a table in under an hour without looking at the instructions (multiple things I cannot do) and I still wouldn't feel as butch as when I'm on top of some dude, fucking him. It's the domination, the power of it all. It's fulfilling the traditional masculine role—with a twist! But as a self-proclaimed sissy, someone who actively avoids traditional masculine roles, it's a little weird. Am I a masc? Is this how it starts? Should I start saying "bro" and "dude" *unironically?*

The biggest turnoff for me in the whole unholy hookup dance of dating apps is when some random fag messages me, "Hey bro." Or, "Sup dude?" My first instinct is always, *Ma'am. Who are you trying to impress?* 'Cause it ain't me. I'd much rather be greeted with a "Hey gurl" or "Sup kween?"

Now, there are gays lumbering around a Home Depot somewhere genuinely calling each other "bro" and "dude," and I'd gladly fuck them. They'd also probably let you know that they're naturally masculine, to put to rest any lingering doubt over it—your doubt, their doubt—and would prefer if you were, too.

They try to find ways to reinforce their own masculinity. This might be a rejection of the "gay lifestyle"—"I'm not into the scene," he says, meaning he's not out in gay bars or clubs, vacationing at Mykonos and Fire Island, listening to Beyoncé or Taylor or the pop diva du jour. He may watch *Drag Race*, but he can't name any of the queens . . . unless expressly asked. Then he'll go into a ten-minute tirade on who should've won this season or that. Because *Drag Race* is gay professional sports. Seriously, there are fantasy leagues and everything.

For these gays, being a sissy (outside of *Drag Race*) isn't good fun; it's repulsive. It's too stereotypically gay. It riles their own internalized homophobia and therefore must be avoided. Lest there be any lingering doubt over one's perceived masculinity or presumed heterosexuality.

TOPPING MADE ME feel like the man I was supposed to be, virile, erect, a bearer of seed. I used to lean in to the macho element, growling at my partner, "Whose ass is this?" That never felt quite right coming out of my big gay mouth, but I thought that was what tops said! Bottoms, it seemed, wanted aggressive, masculine, dominant tops. That seemed like a lot of work on my part. Not as much work as the bottom put in, mind you, but playing at masculinity was still a stretch.

But just the act of topping was like naturally embracing my own masculinity. There was no need to add artifice. In turn, blasting dudes made me more comfortable in my own masculinity, or lack thereof. Yes, I like to wear wigs and twirl around to peak '70s Diana Ross, but at least I'm not taking a dick up my ass. Which, again, not for lack of trying.

If topping makes me feel totes masc, then does bottoming make others feel emasculated? Not like that feeling of emasculation would ever stop a gal from bottoming. I don't know if you've ever met the average bottom, but they *really* enjoy their work. Bottoming, after all, is supposed to be a passive act. But then you try fucking a bossy power bottom and tell me who's in control.

And just considering the pain of being penetrated, it takes a real man to be a bottom. Yet the prevailing wisdom among the gays is not necessarily that a bottom is femme, but a femme is always expected to be a bottom—to fulfill the traditional feminine role—or at least vers. Just as tops are expected to be masc, fulfilling the traditional masculine role.

NO MATTER HOW nontraditional gay men are, or feel, or are made to feel, we tend to relegate ourselves into traditional, binary roles—masculine and feminine, top and bottom, Britney and Christina—in order to feel part of a hierarchy that otherwise excludes us. The expectations that we place on ourselves and on one another can then explain a tendency to overcompensate. Some of us feel that we need to address the ways we've failed to live up to society's expectations of performative masculinity.

Without much choice in the matter, being on the outside can make one want to be on the inside all the more. So if the bottom is the effeminate role, she might start dropping that voice an octave just for the chance of getting someone inside her.

Then there's the weight of expectation of just being a man and all the shit that that means. A time comes in every gay man's life when he will have to butch it up. Either for his parents, or his friends, or his school, or his job, or that hot guy with the beard and flannel shirt who looks like he just stepped off a paper towel package.

More than a sexual kink, performative masculinity has traditionally been a survival instinct. Gay men used to have to pass as straight to get by in the world. Those who didn't were ostracized. Or killed. In Gore Vidal's *The City and the Pillar*, the main character, Jimmy Willard, while an unashamed homosexual, is unimpeachably masculine. In the book's climax, Jimmy is reunited with his teenage love Bob, who is now married and living a traditional heterosexual lifestyle.

Jimmy wants to be with Bob, but Bob doesn't want to be perceived as gay and punches Jimmy. The two fight, and Jimmy, the stronger and thus more masculine of the two, wins, and to assert his dominance, he rapes Bob. Jimmy robs Bob of his precious masculinity. This is especially significant because Jimmy Willard is one of the first gay protagonists not to die or be killed off by the end of a narrative.

The 1948 novel seems to implicitly say that in order to survive in this world as a homosexual, one has to be unimpeachably masculine. Originally Vidal had meant for Jimmy to kill Bob, which was too melodramatic even for him. Rape is about power, however, and Jimmy takes Bob's power, his masculinity, and walks away without any repercussions. And he's supposed to be the hero. Faggots would continue to die and be villains in various fictions for the rest of the century, but Jimmy Willard, noted rapist, would always be one of our first heroes.

The gays, always adept at survival, assimilated masculinity and then fetishized it. The most stalwart icons of American manliness—the cowboy, the sailor, the soldier, the biker—were all sexual fodder for Tom of Finland's homoerotic art and also made up the majority of the Village People. But the Village People, and to an extent Tom of Finland, are campy takes on masculinity, masculinity with a wink. Tom of Finland exaggerates the masculinity of his subjects; he exaggerates their bulbous pecs, their bulbous packages. His art is an exaggeration of masculinity, and yet gay men accepted it and adopted it *as* masculinity.

What actually passes for masculinity among gay men varies, but it can often be unintentionally campy. Take leather daddies, for instance. When I see a leather daddy, even out of leather, I immediately know he's a faggot. It's the exaggeration of his masculinity that gives it away. The withering muscles or the handlebar mustache or the piercings or the tattoos and maybe the outline of a cock ring in his jeans. That archetype is an obvious signifier to those in the know. But it's based on this hypermasculine ideal.

I feel like gay men who have a real hard-on for masculinity take part in a kind of unconscious drag, embodying their idea of masculinity and taking it to the floor. Fives, fives, fives across the board. There's this one section of John Rechy's *City of Night* that's always stuck with me, involving a big, muscular, macho leather daddy who's drinking and, as the night goes on, becomes more and more of a kween, and the narrator gets more and more repulsed by him. That was what I thought masculinity was in the gay community. A facade. A joke we were all in on. Only as I got older did I realize that masculinity wasn't a facade, but a game, one in which I could choose to play or not.

WHEN I USED to go out with my sisterssss, I would dress like a faggot on a mission, and that mission was to *turn it*. But I knew, and so did my gays who also liked to turn a lewk, that if one wanted to get laid, one would have to "dress like a boy." How boring. Now, I might flip the brim of my cap to the back to offer a little jock post-warm-up tease, though I can't catch a ball to save my life. I'll likely drop the "gurls" and "ma'ams" from my vocabulary if talking to a man I have hopes of seeing naked. I'll do any number of things to seem less gay than I actually am, but I draw the line at the dance floor.

I love to dance, and I love to dance like a bad bitch with the rent due. At least I did before my knee surgeries. Now I dance like an old Black man, which is to say beautifully. But in my gayheyday, I was throwing it back like an old-school joint. Sweeping my ass across dance floors all over this great land of ours. Popping that pussy for Jesus. Dropping down, getting multiple eagles on, kweening out for the love of dancing, for the love of my friends, for the love of being alive. Too alive. I was too much. Too gay.

At a certain point, going out to bars and clubs became untenable. Queer I'd be, dressed like a boy, dimming my light, barely moving my hips, eyes darting around like a fiend, on the prowl for some ass, and having a terrible time. Why go out?!

The only gays I ever see dancing with full abandon anymore are the middle-aged lesbians in Provincetown during Solid Gold Tea. Those gals get it! Gay dance floors now are often too crowded with people just standing around, looking cute, trying to look butch, trying to catch someone's eye, unaware that the sexiest thing a person can do is dance, no matter how good or bad. Well, there are limitations on just how bad you can be, but at least have fun. The dance floor, after all, is the holiest of places for my people, the faggots who leave their bodies when the right song comes on; it is the cradle of joy. Therefore, I would never disrespect the dance floor by refusing to pay tithes with my thighs.

FOR KWEENS WHO completely eschew airs of masculinity, who thrill in being femme bottoms but are nonetheless attracted to masculine men, there are big, burly men who will gladly wife them up, and I love to see it. What's a more patriotic image than a giant macho daddy and his bossy little twink husband, living the American Dream? These traditionally masculine men may find a femme partner more in line with their traditional views of relationships. They're the man of the house, even if they might be the bottom of the couple.

But what of femme tops? The blouses. You see them blowing in the wind from time to time. The ladies who thrust. Thin as a reed with a dick fatter than a soda can. Or just a sister who loves doing it for herself. The blouse, however, risks rejection because her perceived femininity could make an already insecure, internally homophobic, and possibly misogynistic bottom all the more so. Hence why we have the popular refrain "masc for masc." It's just a little shorthand to avoid any purses falling out of mouths or other orifices. It's also, I find, pretty offensive. And I'm an offensive person. By nature, by will, by hook and by crook.

On the one hand, I get it. You know what you like, you don't want to waste your time, we're all busy working gals of the go-go '80s. But on the other hand, it just seems so silly. You're setting some random standard for masculinity that both you and a potential partner have to meet, and in order to do so, you strive to out-butch each other. At least until the day you let loose a Gaga lyric in casual conversation and it all goes to hell in the handbag that just fell out of your mouth. Silly.

Masculinity is just *silly* to me. As a concept. But that's from my personal experience. I come from a background where boys were expected to act like boys, from a culture, West Indian, that doesn't much care for sissies. I was a sissy, but it wasn't beaten out of me. A lot of gay men come from traumatic backgrounds, where their masculinity was armor against abuse or derision or being found out.

The long and terrifying history of violence against gay men no doubt plays a significant part in our collective obsession with masculinity. Another significant part is America's collective obsession with masculinity. The man's man is a major tenet of the American myth: the pioneers, the cowboys, the rugged individualism, the strong silent type, and all that gay shit. I mean, is there a gayer saying than "a real man's man"?

That's supposed to be a compliment for the most macho among us, but "a man's man" just sounds to me like the theme of a gay wedding invite. "A Man's Man: Please join Keith and Kieth on their journey to forever this June."

There seem to be a lot of people who would rather things go back to how they were. Straight men—straight white men, especially—are really going through it. They have their own distinct idea of what it means to be a man, and I am *not* it. In fact, their brand of manhood is endangered, and they're here to protect it. That kind of rhetoric is so . . . gay. Like, if you love being a man so much, why don't you marry one? But the thing is, masculinity is attractive to gay men and straight men alike.

I didn't use to understand why men found someone like Donald Trump "a man's man." Physically, he didn't have it. But I view masculinity in physical and sexual terms. Straight men view masculinity as a physical aspect, yes, but also a behavioral aspect. The fact that Trump could, ostensibly, say and do whatever he wanted, without repercussion, and demand respect (not that he got it, but it was demanded, loud and often) made him a masculine ideal. This, despite his glaring lack of physical prowess.

He was also accused of sexual assault by multiple women, accusations that have felled other men. But the boys' clubs of august American institutions from the Ivy League to Wall Street to the federal government have long concealed, if not endorsed, sexual assault. Rape was the purview of their power as men. The #MeToo movement somewhat rattled the systems that absolved these men, but Trump was a notable exception. Embodying the most toxic elements of masculinity, he became an icon of American men.

This, after years of masculinity being challenged and redefined in the public sphere. Or, well, this reassertion of an old ideal was *a result* of masculinity being challenged and redefined. Making America great again also meant making men *men* again, going back to traditional gender roles, away from transgender this and gender nonbinary that. Men en masse had felt they had to start *apologizing* for being men, and though the apology was long overdue, they were shooketh with fear and confusion, which inevitably led to anger.

Since when did being a man become a bad thing? About the same time that men started to oppress women. Trump represented the old guard of masculinity, unapologetic, uncompromising. He felt out of step with the culture I was experiencing in my queer, diverse, gender spectrum'd, big-city life, but America is built on contradicting ideas. All men are created equal, just not their slaves. Or women. Or the Irish. The progression and acceptance of once-radical ideas can serve as a bulwark for the still-traditional ones.

MAGA GAYS ARE a true curiosity. Log Cabin Republicans have been sulking in corners since 1977, when a bunch of white kweens in California banded together to stop the Briggs Initiative, which proposed banning homosexuals from teaching in public schools. They had a dull sheen of respectability despite actively going against their own interests time and time again, candidate after candidate. But the MAGA gays are like all MAGA adherents: immune to reason.

Gays for Trump were the subject of interest and jokes . . . lots of jokes . . . in 2016, when they backed the future forty-fifth president. That there are still faggots who support Trump after he spent four years actively dismantling LGBTQ+ rights is curiouser and curiouser still.

When Trump told a Gay for Trumper that they didn't "look gay" at a 2022 rally, the group's founder insisted it was a compliment, telling *Newsweek* that a GfT'er "probably wouldn't 'look gay' because it's a stereotype that fits more with the typical 'look' of leftist LGBT."

He's got a point. The leftist fags love a rainbow. Too much, some would say. He then added, "Not saying some of us might look fabulous and 'gay.'" Trust me, sis, no one looks fabulous at a Trump rally.

You'd think gays would be immune to MAGA fever, and while most queers do lean left, the desire to be part of a club that wants nothing to do with you is typical self-loathing-minority behavior. One might assume that all MAGA gays are white, but wouldn't you know it: I accidentally hooked up with a Black one.

It *was* an accident. I had no idea who he was when he messaged me on Grindr. He said he was a dancer, he was cute, he had a nice butt, and he was pretty insistent, so I invited him over one day. He was very nice; we had a good time. I saw him on Grindr again and decided to follow his Instagram. I didn't actually look at his Instagram, but in case I wanted to sleep with him again, I wanted to seem interested in his life or whatever.

I was about to post a nice message on his birthday when I actually scrolled through those little squares. This nigga. This faggot. He was vehemently pro-Trump, espousing MAGA ideas, trolling and owning the libs, friends with Fox News commentators. I immediately unfollowed. I was shooketh. I just did not expect to find a Black MAGA gay; it's like the opposite of a unicorn. Some ungodly chimera made entirely of conflicting bad decisions.

He didn't remotely fit the typical example of a Trump supporter. Black, gay, kind of effeminate. He was a dancer and a cheerleader, definitely not like the white masc-for-masc MAGA fags I'd encountered in the past. And I was further surprised that he was into me, a Black boy, because I thought that he would naturally be into white boys. Like, what Black gay is wifing him up? I'd sincerely like to know, out of pure curiosity and, of course, shade.

I would think a conservative Black gay would be conservative throughout. And for Black men, even the gay ones, masculinity is a sacred tenet, one that has been under attack for some four hundred years.

BLACK MASCULINITY IS something that both Black men and Black women can be very protective of, considering the history of the emasculation of our men. Both literal and figurative. As enslaved people, men were sold off from their families, raped by their owners, both male and female, and sometimes castrated as a punishment. After slavery, Black men were routinely lynched with their dicks stuffed in their gaping mouths.

Black men had to suffer being called "boy" by white men younger than them in front of their wives, in front of their kids. They suffered the indignities of employment discrimination, working harder and earning less than their white counterparts, and always at the heels of the white man.

Black women, in turn, took on as their duty the preservation and protection of the vestiges of their men's manhood, just so he could make it out into the world another day. Black men's frustration with their lot in life, and its generations of forced separation gnawing at their bones, sometimes led to violence, to abandonment, to just giving up.

Black masculinity has been under attack, most prominently by the very nation that promised equality only to rescind the bargain. Homosexuality used to be seen as just another attack on Black masculinity, because it undermined the Black family, as exalted by the Black church, the pillar of the Black community. I say "used to" because while there are still very homophobic attitudes perpetuated by the Black church, Black gays of faith are numerous. The church may have rejected them, but they didn't reject the church. And then there are the Black churches that accept them as they are.

I'm very glad I grew up in a relatively nonreligious house. Religion was never my thing or my mom's. It was more my aunt's thing, and I tagged along to church for the smell of frankincense and myrrh, the gorgeous stained glass windows, and the brunch after Sunday service. But if I had grown up religious, I might have had more conflict with my sexuality, having been taught how egregious a sin it was.

That kind of indoctrination really fucks up Black gays, who already struggle with the societal prejudices that are set against them. Now they have to worry about going to hell, too? Hell? They know her. They live there. And heaven help them if they're a sissy. In the pilot episode of *Empire*, Lee Daniels's audacious soap about a powerful Black family in the music industry, Lucious Lyon (played by Terrence Howard) infamously stuffs his gay son into a trash can after catching him in his mother's heels.

It was based on a real incident that happened to Daniels. "He put me in a trash can and he said that I would never be nothing," Daniels told *Ebony* in 2014. "He said, 'You already have it bad, boy, 'cause you're Black—now you're a faggot, too.'" For conservative or religious Black parents, having a child who is gay on top of being Black seems like a choice, as if they're choosing to make their life harder. But who would choose that?

Because their masculinity is such a precious commodity that is constantly under attack by outside forces, Black men can adopt a hypermasculine posture. Growing up in Poughkeepsie, I saw boys who I knew were sensitive and sweet getting into fights and joining gangs just to prove how tough they were, to avoid becoming victims. Poughkeepsie gangs weren't shit, but there was the pressure to be a man when they were still boys.

Their ideas of being a man, however, were a problem in and of themselves.

I always thought Black masculinity was violent. Never tender. Never fatherly. Never loving. I didn't grow up with a father, so I got my education in Black masculinity from the media . . . and I guess my uncle and brother. On the one hand, I was taught that being a man meant being responsible, being a good TV dad, a good TV son. In a very special talk during a very special episode, TV Dad might tell TV Son that having a gun (TV Son brought a gun to school!) doesn't make him a man. Choosing not to use it does. Cue audience applause.

On the other hand, rappers were the idols of my peers, and their idea of manhood was violent, misogynistic, and homophobic. But dammit if a banger isn't a banger. Some of the sickest couplets in rap history are also homophobic as fuck. To wit, the Notorious B.I.G.'s 1997 classic "Hypnotize," where he brags, rather hypnotically, about putting "hoes" across this great land of ours—from NY, Miami, DC, and Philly—onto

DKNY, Versace, and Moschino while warning of "them niggas" who "ride dicks."

I was eleven or twelve years old, rapping along to that song (well, trying to rap along—the dexterity in those lines is next level), all the while fully aware of what he meant by niggas riding dick. Some of my favorite songs growing up were blatantly homophobic, with overzealous use of "faggot" to describe gay men or men who fell short of their masculine ideals. "Pussy" was another one. Pussy-ass niggas. Rap influenced the style, the attitudes, the language of my peers. And I was a pussy-ass nigga.

For all its hypermasculine posturing, I always found rap . . . kinda gay. Especially because of the hypermasculinity. So much of rap consisted of drag: the highly gendered posturing, the opulence, the furs and jewels. Before the '80s, only white women wore that much fur and diamonds. Now every emcee with a deal is walking around looking like Alexis Carrington Colby. There was a definite shift in the culture when, in 2002, East Harlem rapper Cam'ron showed up to a Baby Phat fashion show in a baby-pink fur coat and matching hat. Black men started wearing the traditionally "girly" pink because it looks stunning against our skin, and also because Killa Cam made it cool. Decades later, that image is emblazoned on T-shirts, sandals, bags, you name it. Rappers were able to both define and defy masculinity.

Even homophobic lyrics had a homoerotic tinge. "Should I smack him with my dick and the mic?" DMX asks of niggas who think they're Superman, reminding them he has the Kryptonite (apparently his dick) on the certified 1999 banger "Party

Up." Considered one of the hardest rappers to ever do it, DMX had a real boner for gays.

"Last I heard, you cowards was havin' sex with the same sex," he rhymes on the get-the-Glock-ready anthem "Where the Hood At." Later, in the same verse, he ponders, "How you gonna explain fucking a man?" then concludes, "Even if we squash the beef, I ain't touchin' your hand," then admonishes "chumps" in jail wearing "Kool-Aid on his lips and pumps."

To further illustrate his point, Dark Man X features in the music video two sissy jailbait fags flanking a real daddy type, and on the pumps line, one of them flashes a kitten heel. Bitch, if that isn't camp, I don't know what is.

One of the *gayest* music videos I have ever seen, limp wrists down, is DMX's "Ruff Ryders, Anthem," which is about as hard as rap can get. In the video, X is shirtless surrounded by a bunch of also-shirtless jacked dudes in a prison yard, baggy jeans sagging under their asses, hyping one another up, pushing one another around, lifting weights in their Timbs. All I saw were some jacked dudes getting off on one another. If they were white and those jeans were sagging all the way down to their ankles, this could be Fire Island or Mykonos. That video was so masculine it was flaming gay.

Rap loves to overplay its masculine hand. But there's also a winking knowingness to the faggotry of it all. Biggie was long rumored to have ghostwritten Lil' Kim's lyrics, and proof seemed to surface in 2008. A demo leaked on the internet of Kim's proto-bad-bitch manifesto "Queen Bitch" from her debut album, 1996's *Hard Core*, with Biggie spitting the lyrics.

The producer of the track, Carlos Broady, told *Rolling Stone* in 2020 that the beat was originally intended for Biggie, but record executive and occasional genius Sean "Puff Daddy" Combs, who was also the Brooklyn rapper's executive producer, rejected it on Biggie's behalf. Biggie, however, wanted to keep it for a new artist, Kimberly Jones, aka Lil' Kim, and wrote and recorded a rough demo of "Queen Bitch" over the rejected beat, leaving it on Broady's answering machine.

Hearing the late rapper deftly rhyming about "buffoons eating my pussy while I watch cartoons" and how he's gonna "stay that bitch" in his husky baritone adds a whole other layer to the bad bitchery birthed from *Hard Core*. After all, as a gay man, I could relate to a female rapper and rap along to her lyrics and feel like an empowered bad bitch, too. To think a man wrote that, one of the most respected and feared rappers of all time, is subtly mind-blowing to me. That's drag, that's camp, that's gay rights.

Gay rappers today are basically just aping Lil' Kim and Foxy Brown—whose lyrics on her debut album, *Ill Na Na*, were co-written by none other than Mr. Beyoncé, Jay-Z. Saucy Santana is out here in these streets rapping about pussy and Prada like he's in a lime-green fur and matching wig. And he just might be. And he just. Might. Be.

Women gave gay rappers and gay rap lovers an entry point into a genre that could often be homophobic and hypermasculine. That a few of the most homophobic and hypermasculine rappers themselves helped write some of those game-changing lyrics just speaks to the oft-contradictory nature of obsessive masculinity. Biggie, however, will forever stay that bitch. In my heart.

AS A BLACK gay man interacting with non-Black gay men, I found that my masculinity was usually presumed. That I was Black and muscular provided me with a preliminary masc-for-masc background check. The idea of the Mandingo, the well-endowed Black man ravaging a white woman, is still popular among white Americans, despite being a decades-old trope, dating back to the 1957 novel of the same sensational name.

I used to chafe at the presumption, that I had to live up to this Black masculine ideal that I could never possibly meet. With every hookup I feared being found out as a fraud, a sissy in stud clothing. What if I wasn't masculine enough for him? What would betray me? I thought I had to butch it up to be desirable, but I also felt that I had more pressure to be butch than a white man. I had to be more masculine because I was Black, and to a white boy, that meant I was more than man; I was Mandingo.

To deter that kind of interaction, I began making sure to state my own indifference to others' masculinity as well as my own. Others did the same, yet the masc-for-masc bros remained. If one of them asked me if I was masc, I'd reply ambivalently, "Sure, I guess?"

I like faggots. I like fucking faggots. I love hooking up with a guy and fagging out about Jane Krakowski's splits on Broadway in *She Loves Me*. She does a split and is dragged across stage . . . *while still in the split*. I want to have sex with people who appreciate that. And it's just more freeing when both of us aren't hung up about appearing as masc as possible to each other, draining the fun out of what should be a fun experience.

As I've gotten older, I've grown more comfortable with my own masculinity, or lack thereof. Yet, despite my best intentions, I've evolved into a daddy. That mostly consists of my being tired all the time. But I've also aged into a certain kind of manhood. My body has changed, and with it my movements and postures have changed as well.

I can't drop down and get my eagle on anymore, for one. Thanks to my torn ACL and meniscus, I'm currently not able to dance like the carefree faggot of my youth. I'm quite sad about it. If I'm not popping my figurative pussy, am I truly alive? I also can't switch like I used to. Naomi Campbell used to have nothing on me. Well, she did, but I had some stems, too, dammit. Now I can only waddle and wobble, Weeble-like. My body has forced me to embrace masculinity by betraying me.

And then there's my fashion. I used to work in fashion, turning gender-fluid lewks, squeezing my size-tens into whatever shoes I could find. I found them at Payless. And yes, it did feel good. I can't wear a heel anymore. The last time I tried was in Provincetown, during the annual Drag Brunch, when locals and visitors alike doll up and parade their best lewks. I powered through with some modest hooker heels, but I had to take them off on the way home. It was a low moment for me. I had yelled at drag queens for making the same fashion faux pas. Once, at Fag Bash, the party that follows Drag Brunch, I had rolled both ankles while in six-inch stilettos. I still wore my heels all the way home.

If I do drag again, what am I gonna wear? A wedge? I'd

rather stay home. What's more, I've taken to exclusively wearing Crocs—my twentysomething self would open-palm slap me at even the suggestion. If there's a universal sign for giving up, that's it. Sure, I'm still the same faggot on the inside, but I can't fully express myself as I used to, and I feel more masc for it. No one ever told me aging would turn me into a man.

Comfortable shoes, however, are pretty nice. And I no longer squeeze myself into something because it looks good. I'm fine with just sweats, anywhere, anytime. But the best part of being a daddy—that is, a sexy older gay—is meeting younger (legal-aged) boys who like older men. I don't mean that in a predatory way . . . well, more predatory than interactions between all gay men are, regardless of age, since nearly all of us are horndogs who would run over a disabled orphan for some, at best, decent dick. But I've always had a daddy fixation. I wanted an older man to make me feel safe, who would take care of me.

All the daddies I pursued were white. I could never bring myself to sleep with an older Black man because that hewed far too close to my actual daddy issues. And for some reason, I've had daddies call me "son" on occasion, which I do *not* find *at all* sexy. To be called that by someone who could plausibly be my dad while I'm inside him would ruin sex for me, and ruin just being alive, for the rest of my life. It's not that I wanted these white men to be my father, but there was just something so comforting in calling another man "daddy."

But that comfort has been supplanted by other guys calling *me* daddy. I don't have what one would call a "nurturing" nature by any measure, but having craved a daddy figure for all my gay youth, I've gladly assumed the role for other baby gays, to provide them what I could never find. I am my own daddy. It has nothing to do with incest but rather power. Daddy is in charge. And I like being able to be in charge of something in my life, even if it's a chaotic twink.

Age gaps had allowed me a degree of submission that I otherwise couldn't experience as a top. Bottoms can submit to a top and feel taken care of. Being a top was a lot of pressure. Sometimes I just liked being told what to do. I wanted to feel taken care of. And older men loved telling me what to do. Even when I wasn't sleeping with them. Older men also appealed to me because they were more likely to know what they wanted and were able to get my references. You'd be surprised how many twenty-two-year-olds have never heard of Rosalind Russell.

Furthermore, for a young gay man with a hard-on for gay history, the daddy/son dynamic was a tale as old as time. Take the Sacred Band of ancient Thebes, 150 pairs of male lovers that served as the city's secret weapon against the bellicose Spartans in the fourth century BCE. Each couple comprised a daddy and a son, an older man and a younger man. The idea behind the army was that these warriors would be emboldened by their lovers and their devotion to each other, so much so that in the heat of battle they would rather fight to the death than lose face in their lover's eyes.

For decades they went undefeated, until their forces were outmanned and destroyed by Philip II of Macedon in the Battle of Chaeronea in 338 BCE. The Sacred Band were buried together, 150 pairs of graves, with some skeletons later found holding hands. Awwww. Dead gay lover bones.

Apart from the sexual side of things, older gays have a treasure trove of wisdom on being gay men, and it was always nice to pick their brains, to hear about gay New York in the '90s, or '80s, or '70s. Absent a father figure, a gay elder, I thought, could teach me what it was to be a gay man. Now that I am becoming a gay elder, I have no idea. I have nothing to share with the younger gays about masculinity, except that it's a bore to obsess over it. But they seem to be figuring that out on their own.

When I log on to the apps today, the gurls are out. Blouses are just billowing beautifully. I used to be worried about guys being turned off by my wearing nail polish in my profile pictures. Now boys, gay and straight and anywhere in between, are painting their nails like it's not a big deal. 'Cause it's not. And the apps have adopted a collection of pronouns and gender identities so that users can identify how they feel comfortable. There's so much more out there than masc for masc. And the guys still beating that drum seem almost like knuckle-dragging Neanderthals. And that can be hot, too.

THERE ARE MYRIAD examples of manhood, and how lucky are we, all humans, for that? That all these different ways to be a man, to be human, to be alive, may not be "accepted" but exist nonetheless. We can be privy to this diversity of gender expression should we wish, or some can ignore them, if that's what works for them.

My existence as a faggy butch kween top doesn't threaten that of some hypermasculine alpha bro. If he does feel threatened, maybe we should make out. I'm just saying!

Sometimes that pent-up anger is just pent-up sexual frustration. And in my experience, a dick can . . . go a long way.

5

THE IMPOSSIBILITY OF LOVE

I OFTEN WONDER what I did in a past life for my love life to be as punishing as it is in this one. It must have been terrible, because it does feel like a punishment. An intentional, pointed punishment designed to really get my gander. The lack of romance in my life has been a source of such great pain that I just have to laugh at it . . . you know, to keep myself from crying.

I used to believe in True Love™ and Soulmates™ and all the things great pop songs are made of. I used to believe I could be the heroine of my own romantic comedy, a young Black boy imagining himself a grown-ass white woman.

MY FAVORITE ROM-COM has always been the greatest rom-com, *The Philadelphia Story* from 1940. The film that saved Katharine Hepburn's faltering acting career was based on the play by Philip Barry, and in it Hepburn stars as the imperious, impossibly sophisticated, and *thin* socialite Tracy Lord. She's a bitter divorcée careening her way toward a second marriage, this time with a "man of the people," George Kittredge, played by John Howard. But her ex-husband, C. K. Dexter Haven (played by Cary Grant), sticks his gorgeous nose into the proceedings, trying to save Tracy's father and family from a damaging tabloid story by giving the tabloids a different story, "The Philadelphia Story": the inside scoop on Tracy's wedding.

Tracy, deathly allergic to bullshit, catches on almost immediately but plays along with Dexter's ruse to save her family's reputation. Enter hardened, cynical writer Macaulay "Mike" Connor (played by Jimmy Stewart) to secretly document the wedding. Over the course of the film, Tracy's taken down several notches, by Dexter, who accuses her of being distant and thus responsible for his turning to drink; by her father, who has the nerve to cite Tracy's lack of affection as a reason for his flight to an affair with some jezebel dancer in New York; and by Mike, who calls her out on her patronizing, upper-class snobbery.

The usually puritanical Tracy, facing a crisis of identity, gets drunk on champagne, to the chagrin of her image-conscious and very proper fiancé, George. Then, in one of my favorite scenes in all of film, Tracy and Mike sneak away from her engagement party to dance and banter by the pool. Mike, despite the blue-collar everyman chip on his shoulder, sees a side of Tracy that she doesn't allow many, if anyone, to see.

"You're lit from within, Tracy," he intones. "You've got fires banked down in you, hearth fires and holocausts!" Tracy, tears in her eyes, asks Mike, "I don't seem to you made of bronze?"

She had been compared to a statue, cold and unfeeling, by Dexter, by her father, and, as a compliment, by George. Her fiancé wanted to worship her like a goddess, while Dexter resented her and divorced her for being as distant as a goddess.

"I don't want to be worshipped," she tells George, embarrassed at her own candor. "I . . . I want to be loved."

She's not cold, distant, unfeeling, unalive in Mike's eyes. She's "full of life and warmth and delight." Tracy, overcome with emotion, kisses Mike . . . on the eve of her wedding.

That's what I thought love was. Transformative, poetic. Beautifully lit, written, and acted. I always felt like Tracy, cold and distant. Her father accused her of holding others to the same impossibly high standards to which she held herself. She has this hard exterior that keeps people at a distance as a means to protect herself. But everyone just thinks she's a bitch.

Around middle school I stopped showing emotion. I had been made fun of for crying too many times. Bullies had targeted me for being effeminate. I didn't want to get hurt anymore. I felt things so intensely sometimes my whole body would shut down.

I had discovered the deadpan heroine Daria on MTV, a depressed, bespectacled, deeply cynical, and sarcastic nerd who was never a victim. She was too smart and quick and cutting for that. I saw myself in her, and so I modeled myself after her. I would be emotionless, cold, distant.

I didn't want to be that sensitive, that weak. So I built my cold, expressionless armor, and I learned just how easy it was to turn off my emotions, at least on the outside. Inside I still had fires, hearth fires, holocausts. And so I waited. Waited for someone to come along who would see me the way Mike saw Tracy. Someone who would recognize the warmth and delight beneath the bronze exterior.

I'm still waiting. I've built another set of armor, one of muscle and false confidence, and I can find men to worship me. But I don't want to be worshipped. I want to be loved. Well, actually, I want both.

My junior year in high school, I took an acting class. We had to prepare a monologue from a play to perform in front of the class. The class was like six other kids, all girls, and me. Still, my acting teacher, an English teacher who taught this class as an elective, reserved the entire auditorium for us, so we could have the experience of acting on a real stage. For soft-spoken me, the real challenge was projecting my voice, but I loved performing. And with such a small class, and with all girls, I felt comfortable choosing my monologue and delivering it wrapped in sheets I had brought from home, dressed like a "goddess."

It was the one Dexter gives to Tracy that sets her on her downward spiral of introspection: "I'm contemptuous of something inside of you you either can't help or make no attempt to; your so-called strength, your prejudice against weakness, your blank intolerance." He goes on to tell her she'll never be "a first-class woman, or a first-class human" until she learns to have "some regard for human frailty." Way harsh, Dex.

I was saying Dexter's words, but I was talking to myself. I've had to hold myself to an impossibly high standard in order to just drag myself out of poverty, out of uncertainty, to forge a future of my own, and to live a life on my own terms. Because

I've had to go through some pretty tough shit from a pretty young age, I grew intolerant of those who didn't, those whose lives I perceived were easier or luckier than mine. My strength was forged in fire, and I resented any weakness that remained.

I resented wanting to be in love. I resented having feelings. I wanted to be a pillar of strength for myself, because I thought that all I ever had, or ever would have, was myself. So while I still longed for love, I built defenses against it. "This goddess must and shall remain intact!" Dexter mocks Tracy. I felt that way even in high school, which I spent in the shadow of my mother's death. The fridge always empty, the threat of eviction always hanging over my brother's and my heads. I always felt like an outsider, depressed and lonely, while I watched my friends fall violently in and out of love.

The only thing that kept me going was the promise of getting out of Poughkeepsie, going to New York City, finally getting the chance to be myself, and to fall, *oh to finally fall!*, in love. When I got into one of the most exclusive colleges in the country, I felt validated, positive that I could do anything I put my mind to. And I have made my own way. My eyes are always firmly set on the future; I rarely dwell on the past. I forget sometimes all that I've been able to accomplish when the circumstances seemed impossible.

Why, then, has love been so elusive? Well, to quote the great Janet Jackson, this is a story about control. I can't control how someone else feels. Sadly. Also, I can't control whom I find attractive. I can't control the timing of meeting someone. Love is completely out of my control. And that freaks me the fuck out.

People like me, the Tracy Lords of the world, thrive on control and resent anything and anyone that challenge that control.

I USED TO believe in love. But love is just dumb luck. It's a chance meeting, a moment of shared eye contact, a happy accident that may or may not last. Some of us are lucky, and some of us are not. So far, I've been unlucky. The goddess has remained intact, and the flesh remains cold, unfeeling, but inside, the fires rage. It pains me to say that I want to be loved, to admit to that weakness. I don't cry very often, but when I do, it's usually over that want, that need. It's been a source of such consternation and frustration that it's easiest to just give up on the idea altogether.

But I was made a romantic before I had any choice in the matter, and I still believe in, to my own disappointment, love. That sort of reluctant optimism has, as much as my so-called strength, kept me going. If I didn't believe in a better future, how could I build one for myself? If I didn't believe in love, what was there to believe in? Really. What else is there?

Not being in love can sometimes blind me to the other loves in my life. I didn't get myself out of the hardest times in my life, not single-handedly. I had friends whose love kept me buoyant so I didn't drown in the darkness. I know I shouldn't trade that for the world, but a part of me would to find romantic love. I've joined in mocking those who all but abandon their friends as soon as they find a boyfriend, but secretly I've thought, "Same."

But what if it doesn't work out? Who's left in my corner?

And will it have been worth it? Better to have loved and lost than never to have loved at all.

I thought I was in love once. It felt like it was happening, that I had finally landed in my rom-com, but I couldn't write my own ending. But I can try to write the story on my own terms now.

When Lester Met Dylan

Can two friends not sleep together but
still fall in love in the morning?

MEET LESTER. THE wrong side of twenty-five. Cute, nerdy, body's serving, Black boy with stars in his eyes. Lester's a young writer in the Big City! He's plucky, resourceful, a snazzy dresser, and has a small group of fun, stylish, professional friends. There's Leon, a sassy but sweet casting agent with a taste for the finer couture in life; Leigh, a quirky romantic and model scout at a major agency; and Preston, a slut-on-wheels designer who keeps it real. Too real, some would say.

They treat brunch like a sport, go out dancing multiple nights a week, take annual vacations to Provincetown, where they reliably cause a stir. Life's good, but then, one by one, Lester's friends start finding boyfriends and settling down. They see less and less of one another. Lester is distraught, wanting to find a love of his own.

He knows! He'll log on to the apps. Love's bound to be found a few squares over, only x number of feet away, in a city as big and as gay as New York.

Cut to a montage of bad first dates. Turns out New York is a big city with a small dating pool. Lester is disappointed. Just as he's about to give up, he sees a profile that catches his eye. Unlike the other profiles, this one has . . . pizzazz.

This guy, who's not bad-looking, by the way—he's actually smoking hot, which makes the find that much more appealing—talks about finding someone to duckwalk and death-drop down the street with. He's making multiple references to Lester's personal bible, *Paris Is Burning*. And he's on Jack'd, so he's into men of color. This guy sounds great. He sounds . . . perfect. Could it be, could he be . . . the One?

Lester shoots his shot—"Hey there!"—but doesn't hear anything back. Usually one rejection is enough for him, but this guy seems worth another shot. So a week or two later, he sees him on the apps again and, utilizing those professional writing skills, sends the dream man a funny message. He compliments him on his profile, quotes *Paris Is Burning*, expresses his sincere wishes to get to know him, then holds his breath and presses send.

Lo and behold, the guy writes back. Lester knows that if he can make this guy laugh, he'll be his, so he turns on the charm. They start talking regularly, exchanging phone numbers, texting day and night. The guy's name is Dylan. He works in an office by day and dances on boxes by night. He reads a lot, which Lester finds as attractive as his abs, and doesn't seem burdened by ideals of masculinity that plague other gays.

Lester can feel himself falling for Dylan. He had been waiting patiently, and then there he was. Lester suggests they meet up. Dylan agrees. He invites Dylan to his apartment in

Bed-Stuy, Brooklyn, a small, unimpressive studio that is still all Lester's. Dylan, thankfully, looks like his photos, clearing the first hurdle. For a while Lester feared he might be getting catfished. Again. Dylan could easily be too good to be true. But there he is, standing in Lester's apartment, appraising it and Lester. Lester wonders if Dylan finds him attractive and nervously makes small talk. How he loathes small talk.

Dylan doesn't drink, but he smokes weed, so Lester rolls a few blunts and they start chatting. Lester invites him to a Christmas party (classic!) where the gurls—Leon, Leigh, and Preston—will be. It's one of their traditions, this Christmas party, thrown by this fabulous elder gay who pulls out all the stops. It will be full of attractive gays and model bartenders. Lester is excited to show off Dylan to his friends and to impress Dylan with all the gay fanciness, but when they get there, Dylan appears more uncomfortable than anything.

The gurls are sufficiently impressed, wondering who Dylan is and asking what is going on between them. Lester plays coy, saying they are just friends. But after about thirty minutes, Dylan is ready to leave. Lester wants to stay, but he decides to go with Dylan to Sugarland, a gay bar in Williamsburg, to see where the night will take them, hopefully back to Lester's apartment for some sexytime.

At Sugarland, Dylan starts drinking. A lot. Lester thought he didn't drink, as he had told him several times, but this night is an exception, it seems. Dylan's parents both have alcohol problems, he had revealed during one of their marathon texting sessions, and he had inherited that trait, so he tried to avoid booze. Sometimes he failed.

Some other Black guy is starting to flirt with Dylan. Lester never wants to compete with another Black boy over a white boy—it feels degrading—so he just lets it happen. Dylan is making out with this other guy right in front of Lester, and Lester is getting very upset. He whips out his phone to find someone else on the apps to occupy his time. Dylan, now fully drunk, goes home with the other guy, and a sad Lester slumps home. Lester guesses they're just friends after all.

The next morning, Lester, still sad but determined to not show how upset he truly is, texts Dylan, lying, telling him how nice it was to finally hang out the previous night. Dylan responds hours later. He enjoyed meeting Lester, too. And then he details his night after they parted ways. He was drunk, he says, and he apologizes for that, but not for going home with the other guy. They had sex, Dylan reveals. He was ready to fuck the guy, but he had, in Dylan's words, a "shitty kitty," so he ended up having to get fucked.

This is what friends share, Lester thinks, *so we're just friends. Got it*. Lester tucks away his feelings and resigns himself to a platonic relationship with this boy for whom he had been waiting, it seems, all his life.

But Lester keeps getting mixed signals from Dylan. They spend a lot of time together, talk every day, Dylan starts referring to Lester as his best friend. One day, Dylan observes, "It's like we're dating without the sex," and Lester's ailing heart drops.

Lester goes over to Dylan's apartment before going out to some club so Dylan can do Lester's drag makeup. Dylan, who claims he was raised by drag queens, does some light drag burlesque along with his dancing because it's Brooklyn so why not? He wants to use Lester's face as a canvas to practice his technique. Lester agrees and sits dutifully for two hours as Dylan beats his face. The end result is sickening. They go to this party, which is really just a half-empty gay bar, but their looks are at least appreciated.

The bar starts to fill, and Dylan starts to drink. An hour or so in, and Dylan is all over Lester, kissing him and telling him how beautiful he is. Lester is flattered, but he knows this might not be the real Dylan, or at least not the Dylan that Lester wants him to be. But Lester also thinks back to *The Philadelphia Story* and how getting drunk revealed Tracy Lord's inner feelings and desires. Maybe Dylan feels more for Lester than he originally thought.

Lester doesn't make any moves on Dylan, who's the worse for wear, and as Jimmy Stewart says in *The Philadelphia Story*, "There are rules about that sort of thing." He may have kissed Katharine Hepburn, but he wasn't going to go any further than that.

Like any neurotic New Yorker, Lester is in therapy. He brings up Dylan to his therapist, an older white gay man with a slightly whiter Van Dyke beard. Lester suspects he grew that beard to appear more therapist-like. Therapist drag.

Lester wants to tell Dylan how he feels, but he's never declared his feelings for anyone. Ever. He's had feelings before, and thought guys might share those feelings, but he could never bring himself to say his feelings out loud. His therapist, however, helps him realize that telling Dylan is something he should do—otherwise, he'll always spend his time wondering *what if?*

Lester works up the courage, but he can't say how he feels to Dylan's face. Instead, he writes it. He writes him an email, pouring out his feelings, telling Dylan how much he admires him, how he's waited for someone like him, and how he hopes they can still be friends after this bombshell. Dylan doesn't respond immediately, but eventually he tells Lester that they need to talk.

That can't be good, Lester thinks, *or can it?* He is positive that Dylan has feelings for him, too. It can't all be in his head. Dylan has a date, but before that, he meets with Lester at a bar near Dylan's apartment. Lester is filled with anxiety and fear and hope. Hope above all. But when he sees Dylan, he knows that hope is for naught.

Dylan thanks him for the email, saying it's one of the nicest things anyone has ever sent him. But he doesn't feel the same way. Lester is shattered. This is exactly what he feared would happen. Dylan's sorry. "I know you've waited for me," he says. There's something between them, he continues, but he's not sure what it is. Lester, however, is too sure. He calls Lester the girlfriend he's always dreamed of. Then a conversation he and Dylan had earlier pops up in Lester's mind.

Dylan had told the story then with some trepidation. He was friends with this go-go boy, and he found him very attractive. One thing led to another, and they found themselves on the fast track to fucking, but Dylan couldn't go through with it. This go-go boy, who was so hot and all that, was also too effeminate for Dylan to find completely attractive. And so, they just remained friends. So much for Dylan's supposed enlightenment.

It's fine for him to vocally eschew traditional masculine ideals, but at the end of the day, he still wants a Man, with a capital M, and Lester is just . . . a girlfriend. Lester does not have anything to say. He wants to go home. He wants to crawl into a hole and die. He wants to never feel this way again. Dylan walks him home. Lester wishes he hadn't, but he still thrills at his presence. When they get to Lester's apartment, Lester says bye. Dylan wonders if they can still hang out. Lester says he needs some time. Dylan understands.

Weeks later, Dylan texts him. Lester tries to convince himself he's over Dylan and agrees to resume their friendship. Dylan's friendship does mean a lot to him, and he can't just throw that away. They're friends again, but something is different. Dylan tiptoes around the obvious, Lester's longing. Dylan is dating, but he doesn't share any of the details with Lester. Not that Lester wants to hear them. He's still holding out hope that Dylan might change his mind.

They talk about it every now and then, this thing between them. Dylan compares them to Ross and Rachel on *Friends*. "Does that make me Ross?" Lester asks. Dylan nods silently. "Damn," Lester says, defeated. No one wants to be a Ross. But Ross and Rachel did eventually end up together.

It's summer now. Dylan helps Lester clean up his backyard, and to celebrate actually having a decent outdoor area (in New York!) for the first time since he moved in, Lester throws a party. It soon becomes Lester and Dylan's party, as Dylan inserts himself in the planning. Lester invites all his friends, including his oldest friend, Diana, down from Poughkeepsie.

Everyone's having a good time, and to their eyes, Lester and

Dylan appear to be together. Diana, three shots in, takes Dylan aside and gives him the "You better not hurt my friend" speech she's been waiting to make since high school. The next thing Lester knows, Dylan is leaving the party abruptly, seemingly without reason. When Diana tells Lester what she did, he understands why.

Dylan hadn't seen what everyone else saw, what was so apparent to Diana. And to Lester. Lester and Dylan stop talking for a while.

And now we're entering the final frames, where everything gets pleasantly resolved. In this version, Lester calls Dylan to a meeting and declares his undying love for him and Dylan realizes, finally, that he feels the same way, and they live happily ever after till the credits roll.

IN REAL LIFE, I professed my undying love to "Dylan," and he blew up at me. He couldn't keep going around in circles with me. He wasn't in love with me; he never would be. And I had to accept that. And in order to accept that, we could no longer be friends.

I felt so pathetic after the incident with Dylan. I had followed around like some lovesick puppy a boy who had no idea what he wanted, until he kicked me to the side. It wasn't supposed to be like this. The goddess had stepped down from her pedestal to join the human race, show vulnerability, weakness, and she was punished for it.

But there are different rules with gay relationships. Our relationships are more complicated; our relationships can carry trauma or insecurity around the fact of one's very gayness. I couldn't even get out of the goddamn girlfriend zone. Then there are the racial implications. Dylan liked Black boys; he had been made fun of for dating Black boys and talking like a "wigger" in his native DC. So, like every white boy who likes Black boys, Dylan had preconceived expectations of a potential lover. He didn't date the kind of Black guys who could be his girlfriend.

It was a real shitty experience. As shitty as that random guy's kitty.

Still, I was glad I told the boy. I didn't have to wonder what could have been. Moreover, I was proud of myself for being vulnerable. And I would continue to do so, because otherwise, I could never really fall in love. I had to keep trying.

My Best Friend's Orgy

Can one fuck date lead to fucking forever?

SEQUEL TIME. LESTER is back in the game after some massive heartbreak. He's practicing that time-tested adage about getting over a man by getting under another one. Many ones. Heartbroken, Lester is out here being a heaux.

Though he's ostensibly just trying to have some fun and repair his broken heart, he enters into each hookup with the hope that it'll be something more, that this next guy might be the One. But they only end up being for one night. Lester insists on going on dates with guys instead of just dropping off some dick and leaving when he's done. Lester knows that sometimes one date can lead to forever. Hence the tagline.

Lester's good on dates, funny and friendly, if maybe a little stiff at first, unsure if the guy is feeling him as much as he's feeling them. Since Dylan, he always fears his feelings won't be reciprocated. And so far he hasn't had any luck. He's gone out with some hot guys here and there, tried out some plain old nice guys. He'll go anywhere or try anything; he's just game to meet someone.

The thing is, he'll have a good date—a great date, even—but then nothing comes of it. The guy will lose interest or just disappear into the gay ether. Is it him? Is there something about him that makes guys run away?

He had had one of those great dates with this Eastern European ballet dancer he was crazy about. They got along well, and by the end of the date, they were making out, and cuddling, and holding hands. The ballet dancer had originally said he had no intention of sleeping with Lester; a kiss was barely on the table. But then he wanted to fuck. And so Lester took him back to his place and they fucked.

Lester would always wonder whether if he had just slowed down, demurred, made this beautiful Eastern European ballet dancer wait, things would've turned out differently. But his being a beautiful Eastern European ballet dancer and Lester being a sucker for muscular asses, Lester could not resist.

They had some good sex, but then he didn't hear from the ballet dancer. He texted him after two weeks went by without a word, and the ballet dancer explained that Lester looked him in his eyes too much when they were fucking and it freaked him out. That was just one of the reasons the ballerino twirled away, but it made him question if his desperation was palpable. The dancer had just gotten out of a serious relationship and was hesitant to get into another. Lester had really liked him; he had really liked everyone. But he brushed himself off and kept going.

IT'S SATURDAY NIGHT. Late Saturday night. Lester has a date. The guy was very mysterious about where they were going, but they aren't meeting till one a.m. Lester figures it's a sex party. He's been to his fair share of sex parties, and he has nothing against them; they just aren't his first choice for a first date. But the guy is hot (of course he is), and he's always wanted to go to one of these things with somebody so he doesn't feel the anxiety of going alone. What if no one wants to fuck him? What's sadder than a wallflower at an orgy?

It's raining, and Lester is in Midtown, hell on earth, on his way to meet this guy, Lexey, another Eastern European boy. He is a grad student studying nerdy-ass statistics, but he is built and kinda weird, so Lester is intrigued on numerous fronts. He would prove to this Lexey that he can hang, that he would be a good partner in crime. Wherever the night went, so would he.

Lester meets Lexey at a gay club in Hell's Kitchen. He is instantly attracted to him, despite his warrior faggot uniform of a mesh tank top and camo cargo pants. Lexey is oddly serious. Even for an Eastern European. Maybe he isn't into Lester? They get drinks and take to the dance floor. They're playing that wordless techno crap he hates dancing to, but Lexey seems to love it. Lester puts his arms around Lexey's shoulders, but Lexey promptly removes them.

Okay, Lester thinks. But then Lexey kisses him, dispelling the fears of unreciprocated affection. A few minutes later, he tries putting his arms around Lexey again, and again Lexey removes them. Lesson learned. This Lexey is a strange one, but he's hot (of . . . course he is), and really, isn't that all that matters?

They leave the club and go to a diner to meet Lexey's friends. Meeting his friends already? Where *is* this night going? Lexey's friends are quite nice, nicer than Lexey's been, but he warms up a bit around them. After the diner, the night really starts. As Lester suspected, Lexey's taking him to a sex party. On his dating profile, Lester had remarked that he was a "nice guy, perpetual last-place finisher," and Lexey took that to mean that Lester was the last to finish in an orgy. Lester knew what he was getting into.

The sex party is in some warehouse in Hudson Yards, up a crowded flight of stairs that feels like a fire hazard. Lexey grabs Lester's hand (Lester's heart flutters) and leads him up the stairs, past the crowd, pushing past this Black guy who apparently likes what he sees in Lexey. Finally in the party, Lexey strips down and starts kissing Lester. And everyone else. He has never met someone with such a deranged sex drive. It is on one hand a turn-on, but on the other, Lester watches Lexey fuck and get fucked by strangers up and down that party. So much for a first date.

Yet Lexey always comes back to Lester and kisses on him before running off to continue getting his. Not wanting to be a wallflower, Lester decides to take part in some of the fun himself. Lexey is in heaven, surrounded by jacked Black guys. Lester overhears him say as much when Lexey is talking to one of his (white) friends. Lexey love Black boys, but is that the only reason he's into Lester, since he doesn't seem to have *any* interest in getting to know him?

Lester is having a decent time, he's trying to be a good sport, but he wants Lexey to himself. If he just hangs in there, he knows he'll be able to get him alone. But when it's time to leave the sex party, at seven in the morning, they just head to some faggot's apartment in the East Village. In fact, it's the same faggot to whom Lexey had expressed his Black boy joy. Lester is getting tired, but he wants to prove to Lexey that he can hang. Lester and Lexey show up to the apartment—they're among the first guests—but before long, other party attendees arrive and pick up where they left off.

That Black guy Lester pushed past on the stairs at the earlier party is at this apartment, too. Lester, delirious on drugs of all sorts and trying to enjoy the debauchery, smiles at him, but the guy rolls his eyes and looks at Lester with such disgust his stomach turns. Then Lexey sees the guy, who strips down almost as soon as he gets inside, and starts drooling over him and, of course, fucking him. Lester is no longer having fun. He feels like the lone gay out at the sex party and just hides in the kitchen, moping and feeling sad for himself. Why did he go along with this again?

Lexey doesn't care about him. Suddenly, Lester realizes he's naked, physically and emotionally, and it's time to leave. It might have been time to bail hours ago. He gets dressed and says goodbye to the host, thanking him for having him. Lexey, who has been busy getting fucked, grabs his clothes and tells

Lester he'll walk him out. This comes as a surprise to Lester. He was sure Lexey wouldn't care one way or another.

They end up at a diner across the street, having breakfast together. *Finally*, Lester thinks, *we can have our date.*

Wouldn't it be nice if Lester and Lexey managed to finally have a real conversation and Lexey revealed himself to be a nice guy with real feelings for Lester? A date that leads to forever, instead of what it was: a date that felt like forever. Well, maybe it wouldn't be so nice, as that would hardly excuse all the fucking he did in front of our hero. But Lester knew what he was getting into and could've left at any time.

BUT INSTEAD I stayed. Holding out hope against hope that "Lexey" would pay attention to me for more than five minutes, and when he finally did, he was kind of a dick. He proved humorless and, despite all the wild sex, boring. He was all sex and no personality. It *was* really good sex, though. And of course it was.

Gay men find sex so much easier, and more appealing, than an actual date. Not that monogamous dates are even possible when half, if not like two-thirds, of the men on the apps are in open relationships. Being in a relationship does not preclude one from being a heaux.

So with men either taken or only interested in sex, I often find myself wondering where the hell all the eligible monogamous gays are, or even if they exist at all. Am I one of the last such faggots on earth?

And then I found one.

Bringing Up David

*A screwball comedy about two star-crossed
boys... crossing signals and an ocean*

WE'RE GONNA END this trilogy on a slightly more positive
note. Lester is back, and this time—it's personal. Still un-
daunted in his quest for love, Lester heads to an Oscars party
at the apartment of returning favorite Leon. Their mutual friend
Paul has invited someone named David, whom he describes as
his very muscular British lawyer friend. Lester is intrigued. And
annoyed. Where has Paul been hiding this specimen?

Lester spends the day in Jersey City getting his hair did and
is the last to arrive at Leon's, walking in yelling something or
other. He sees David, and for Lester it's love at first sight. Still,
he plays it cool and says a friendly hello. But David is so handsome and, true to Paul's words, very muscular. He doesn't
drink, which gives Lester echoes of Dylan, and he doesn't
smoke either. *A square*, Lester thinks. *Perfect*.

He's always been attracted to guys who are the opposite of
himself. Dylan and he were too much alike. That may have
been one of the reasons they didn't work out. But how perfect
would it be for Lester, the wacky, free-spirited writer, to take up
with teetotaling David, the human rights lawyer working on his
PhD? It's so *Bringing Up Baby*, with Lester as Kitty Hepburn, as
usual, and David as his Cary Grant. He even has a dimple in his
chin. Lester puts on his most charming pants and sits next to
David. He had made his intentions clear before he even got to
his seat that he wanted David for himself.

They strike up an easy conversation. David is brilliant but silly and doesn't take himself too seriously. He's one of those gays, as is Lester, who restricts carbs but also finds it hard to say no to a good buttered roll. He is undoubtedly a square, but an incredibly attractive one, and there's something between them, Lester thinks. Might as well go for it.

David is overjoyed when *Spotlight* wins Best Picture. Lester hasn't seen it, but David assures him it is a deserved win. David leaves after the ceremony, but Lester stays behind to kiki with the gurls.

"You two seemed to be getting along nicely," Leon says.

"I'm in love with him," Lester says jokingly, but with a kernel of truth.

David is exactly what he wants in a partner. Smart, righteous, buff, kind of a goof. Where has he come from? And again, Paul, where were you keeping him?

Turns out David and Paul had gone on a date, had sex, and decided they'd be better as friends. Lester resents Paul for having tasted the fruit over which he's been salivating, but he also brought David into his life, and they're just friends now, so who cares. It's time for the circle to get the square.

Lester asks Paul for David's email address. The fact that David still has a Hotmail account endears him to Lester all the more. Lester emails David the following day, saying how nice it was to meet him and how interested he is in his work on human rights. And he asks him if he'd ever like to get together.

To his pleasant surprise, David responds that he would love to. They exchange phone numbers and start texting. Lester shares one of the articles he wrote with David, who then goes down a rabbit hole of Lester's writing, coming out the other end effusive in his praise. To Lester's joy and delight, he realizes the two of them have a lot in common.

Paul had said he thought David wasn't very into pop culture, that he was a Luddite who carried a transistor radio, one would assume to pick up the latest news from sixty years ago. David is very much a Luddite, but also, to Lester's pleasant surprise, David is actually a big pop culture junkie.

They could talk about anything, and do, sending voluminous texts back and forth. Lester had initially apologized for the length of his texts until David responded with several pages of his own. It's time to meet again. Lester asks David if he'd like to work out together at his gym. David lives uptown, Lester has moved to Bushwick, but David agrees to make the trek. On a Saturday morning.

He must like me, Lester thinks. *No faggot is making that trip out of the goodness of his heart.*

They meet at his gym in Bushwick, but before he leaves his apartment, Lester cleans up his room just in case David wants to come back after the gym for a different kind of workout. Their conversation is so easy and David pays rapt attention to Lester, not even looking at the other boys in the gym. David further impresses Lester by not only having heard of his home country, Guyana, and not only knowing that it's not in Africa, but having volunteered there a few years back.

Who is this boy? Lester thinks. *Where did he come from? And how can I make him mine?*

Lester is even more impressed by how blissfully unpretentious David is about his looks. He's gorgeous but doesn't seem to care one way or another, not like Dylan, and not like Lester himself. Lester has always been self-conscious about his looks, and to meet a hot white gay who isn't, a true unicorn, feels almost magical. Lester tries to organize more time to hang out with David, who's busy saving the world or whatever, and they meet up a couple times and constantly text.

Lester has fallen. He wants to tell him, but he's afraid, afraid of a repeat of Dylan. But nothing ventured nothing gained; Lester fires off a long text to David, expressing his feelings. David responds shortly afterward. He, too, has feelings for Lester and would love a chance to explore them, but—there's always a but—he's leaving the country in a few months and doesn't want to allow himself the chance to fall for someone knowing that.

Of course he's leaving the country. Lester meets the man of his dreams—and he likes him back!—and he has to leave the country. Can our hero ever catch a goddamn break? David, being British, is in the country studying, but he has to go back after the semester. He loves America and is sad to go, but he knew this would happen. And he's not in a position to start something he can't finish.

Lester appreciates his honesty. And is glad he told David, glad that his feelings were validated, that he wasn't crazy for thinking there was something between him and David.

Lester and David hang out one last time before he leaves. Lester dreams of a fairy-tale rom-com ending, of running through an airport to catch one last glimpse of David before he's out of his life forever, but this isn't a rom-com.

"DAVID" LEFT, AND I haven't seen him since. We still talk all the time. He's a professor at some university in London. I'm still a madcap heiress, just without the money. I can't leave the country because I'm not a United States citizen and I don't have a passport from Guyana, nor can I get one. So I've had to turn down his frequent invitations to come to Europe. But one day I know I'll make it there. And maybe I'll see David again.

Maybe there's a fourth part to this series, where Lester finally gets his man. I'm still crazy about David, but I've accepted that it is what it is. He doesn't seem to be interested in a relationship with *anyone*; he's content to be alone. I try to convince myself of the same, yet I can't convince myself to move on and continue the search. What's the point of wanting anyone else, when I've already found the person I want . . . and I can't have him?

I keep telling myself it's a big world, that I can find someone like David, someone who makes me feel the same way, someone who actually wants to be in a relationship, someone on the same continent. It just feels so . . . unfair. To be tempted with this guy I thought was perfect for me, only for him to be ripped away mere months later.

It feels unfair but also par for the course. Love is all about luck. My luck has never held out, so why would anything be different? But that kind of constant denial makes you bitter. It makes you angry. It makes it harder to love others, to love mankind, to love the world.

THAT BITTERNESS IS why I hate gay rom-coms. Okay, maybe not *hate*. I just can't bring myself to watch any "sunny" gay love story. First of all, the lead guy is never Black and I'm tired of seeing hot white guys fall in love. I couldn't even get into *Fire Island*, a gay retelling of *Pride and Prejudice* with South Korean Joel Kim Booster as an Elizabeth Bennet type and Filipino Conrad Ricamora as a Mr. Darcy type. Because the film takes place in a traditionally very white-gay hot spot.

Provincetown, my gaystination of choice, is also very white, but I'm fond of it mostly for its history as a haven for writers and artists. Ptown feels more like a town of weirdos and outsiders, whereas I've only been to Fire Island once and that was enough. Fire Island has a reputation for being a debauched playground for the white and privileged. My resentment of that world, and of the gay rom-com in general, made me lose all interest in seeing *Fire Island*. I prefer a movie like *Weekend*. Sure, it's about two white gays, but at least it's sad, which is how I feel about dating, and therefore it feels more honest.

In the 2011 film, which was written and directed by Andrew Haigh, who later created the divisive *Looking* for HBO, Russell (played by Tom Cullen) and Glen (played by Chris New) hook up one night. Their evening turns into a fateful weekend relationship right before . . . Glen leaves the country. There are no hijinks or shenanigans. No playful misunderstandings. Russell and Glen fall for each other but have to concede to the limits of reality. And rom-coms are all about defying reality.

At the end of their beautiful weekend, Glen leaves Russell

and the country. And Russell is left with the memory of the weekend, manifested in the tape recorder Glen had been using to document their time together. It's not a happy ending, but it's not a tragic gay story either. It's just heartbreaking, about the seeming impossibility of love among gay men. Which I relate to. I can relate to straight rom-coms because I know they're fiction, I know they're meant to be simple. Those films flatten the characters, their motivations, their complications.

When it's gay characters, I know how messy and complicated and stupid dating other gay men can be. To simplify that is a betrayal of my experience. For which I have bled, literally and figuratively. Gays either loved or hated *Looking* because it attempted to show the messiness, the complexity, the stupidity of dating as a single gay man. Always looking, looking, looking. Though a few more Black characters wouldn't have killed anyone.

The characters in *Looking*, led by Jonathan Groff's Patrick, are self-sabotaging and self-loathing, which some gays found to be a negative representation. Or perhaps a representation too close to home. But I liked it. A lot. It's impossible for the gays to universally like anything that centers them in the narrative, as much as we're always bitching about seeking representation.

When comedian Billy Eichner's rom-com *Bros*, the first gay rom-com from a major Hollywood studio, bombed at the box office, he blamed homophobia, though gay audiences avoided the film like a difficult conversation with their mother. Billed as a traditional rom-com with two gay guys—both white, both boring, neither stars—the film held no appeal for me. If I wanted a traditional rom-com, Clooney and Roberts were going down to Bali. I'll hitch that dumb ride in a minute.

Though I grew up loving traditional rom-coms, I want more from my gay rom-coms. I want diversity, without it feeling like a chore. I want *comedy*, people, *comedy*. Comedy drawn from how shitty it is trying to date. Trying to form a real connection amid casual racism, internalized homophobia, one-night stands, occasional sex parties, drug use and abuse. I want to be able to laugh at the tragedy of my own love life.

It's not fair that our art, rom-coms included, has to be judged by different standards, but we're partly responsible for setting those standards for ourselves. Dating is a gay hell of our own making. Now go make it funny.

6

I HATE THE GAYS

I'VE BEEN SAYING "I hate the gays" for about as long as I've been aware of being gay. It was, originally, a joke. How could I hate the gays when I myself was a gay? Irony, the bread and butter of comedy. But to be fair, I hated everyone. I was a hateful child who grew into an even more hateful adult.

Over time, "I hate the gays" became less a joke and more of a bitter commentary. The phrase became a way to express my disappointment in what I had mistakenly believed to be an inclusive community. I had thought I had found my people, but the people didn't seem to want to include me. My disappointment did not result from some sense of self-loathing or internalized homophobia—quite the opposite. I wanted my community to accept all of us, and all of me, and it kept refusing.

I FUCKING LOVE being gay. Every fag has their own kind of gay, and some kinds are more compatible with others, and some are not. My kind of gay is stereotypical as fuck. I love camp, I love divas (I don't love drag queens, but don't tell anyone), I love show tunes, I live for disco. I will go on long tirades about why a particular actress deserves an Oscar for a specific role that happened decades ago. I pride myself on my taste and on knowing what's tacky and still loving it anyway. This gay essence, in its purest, uncut form, flows through many a kween. This kind of gay is a secret language, it's a shared side-eye, it's kept character actresses working for years. It's a kind of gay that has been passed down from generation to generation, like a cherished heirloom bottle of poppers. It's a kind of gay that transcends race, age, and socioeconomic status. It's a kind of gay that serves as a foundation for the gay community.

To meet someone who loved the same dumb gay shit was to meet a kindred spirit. A meeting of the minds meant there was someone who saw you in a world that erased you or reviled you. The shared connection meant that one would feel less lonely or even feel loved.

Love is one thing, sex is another, and sex ruins everything.

If only gay men could exist in some sexless, platonic fantasia wherein we all sing along to Whitney Houston songs while watching *The First Wives Club* on mute. (We'd pause Whitney for the movie's finale musical number, "You Don't Own Me," *obviously.*) But alas, the threat of sex inevitably arises and sows discord. Resentment, envy, hate.

I don't actually hate the gays. I don't even hate the gay community. But I hate how I feel *in relation to* the gay community, particularly to other gay men. And when I talk about the gays, I almost exclusively refer to white gays.

Of course there have been times when my umbrella of umbrage has shaded the entire queer community in general. But then, unfortunately, it was also easy to conflate the entire gay community with a small subsection of it when that subsection had an outsize influence. My resentment of white gays and their place atop my gay world—because I also lived a very specific gay existence, one defined by whiteness—meant that I didn't feel comfortable in gay spaces, which were predominantly white and catered to whites.

Because I didn't feel comfort in the traditional places where I was supposed to be able to find it—the gay bars and clubs of my forekweens—I didn't develop a sense of community. Instead, I cultivated a resentment of that community and its exclusion of me. Yes, there are Black and Latino gay spaces, but they always feel second-class or like an afterthought or an obligation, such as when a gay bar offers a Blatino night and they beef up the security inside and at the doors. Even spaces that regularly cater to queer people of color have that enhanced air of surveillance, as if Black and brown fags are more violent than white ones. As someone who's witnessed two white twinks get into a slap fight culminating in a *Real Housewives*–esque thrown drink *multiple* times, I can attest that we are not.

But darker skin comes with the expectation of violence, as does a lower economic class, since those Black gay clubs are often in the hood. Even when they're not, the expectation is that the bar will be patronized by poorer people, despite the existence of an exorbitant cover and watered-down drinks. Being Black in the gay community feels more second-class than being Black in America as a whole. In the gay community, you're actually encouraged to settle for separate but less-equal, whether it's a bar, or the apps, or health services. But on the other hand, you're also expected to stand with and support your gay community, unquestioningly, regardless of how your community treats you.

Often, perhaps too often, I used my platform as a writer not to tear down but to call out other gays. White gays. In 2016, I wrote an essay for Out.com about Steve Grand, an openly gay, openly okay singer who was lamenting how people "love" to hate on "young, good-looking, white, gay men."

I wrote that he was right: "We do love to hate young, good-looking, white, gay men. Because they're kind of the worst . . . They sit unfairly at the top of a hierarchy within a minority, mindlessly exerting their influence while ignorant of or indifferent to the world around them, the history before them, and the harm they cause. Their youth, their beauty, their whiteness insulate them from the realities of a world that rewards those qualities in disproportionate amounts. And in the gay community especially, the lack of those qualities strips you of any humanness."

That was when I was still freelancing for *Out*—after a few more essays like that, I got hired full-time. Mine was a perspective that was unique to such a mainstream gay publication at the time. And I clearly didn't give a fuck, which people either loved or hated, but either way, people clicked, shared, and commented.

But it wasn't all calling out basic-ass white gays. I spent years at *Out*, and before at various queer websites, reporting LGBTQ+ news, championing LGBTQ+ issues, shining a light on issues that other (white) writers ignored or didn't know how to approach. As the only Black voice in the room, it was my duty, my obligation, and my burden. If my complicated relationship to white gays is one reason why I "hate" the gays, working in queer media is surely another.

I NEVER STUDIED journalism. The closest I had to an industry education was a journalism class I took my junior year in high school and two years writing for the school newspaper, the *Pioneer Post*. So at my first queer site, *Queerty*, I had to learn on the job, with a loyal and very vocal readership watching. What I learned, early on, was not to read comments on anything I wrote. Anything. No matter how innocuous I thought it was, the *Queerty* readers could always find something to criticize, and it would be something about me, about my character.

I can't recall what the story was, but I had written an article and had done my best to provide both sides to it, because I thought that was what journalists did or were supposed to do, but when I read the comments, one of the readers basically accused me of having a history of being anti-gay. This is when I had barely started, by the way. If they had known me personally, that was a criticism I would've accepted. I can be—and am—openly albeit ironically homophobic around my friends because they know that I am not homophobic in sincerity. If the *Queerty* readers knew how many AIDS jokes I made on a regular basis, I could understand their animosity. You don't make those jokes in mixed company because you don't know how people will react.

Case in point, I was in Provincetown with the gays one summer, having just touched down on the Cape and treading the boards of the pier where the daily Tea Dance was held. There was only a handful of mostly older gays waiting around for the fun to start when a friend of mine got an HIV test at a little pop-up testing site tucked away in the corner. I grew up in the generation for which AIDS was still a very scary prospect, one not yet easily preventable with one pill a day, and so it felt like a curse that we young gays were taught to fear. I was afraid of catching it, and because I was afraid, I made jokes about it. That friend and I had also talked extensively about our sexual practices and our own shortcomings when it came to safe or safer sex.

So after my friend got his test, I started walking over to him but first shouted, from across the pier, "Got AIDS?!" I wanted to make light of the situation and make my friend laugh, which he did. Raucously. Mission accomplished. Though I did hear some disapproving murmurs, as the population of Ptown was decimated by AIDS in the '80s and '90s.

When I got over there, the guy who was offering the HIV tests said bluntly, "Actually, yes. I do."

All my years of practicing Bea Arthur's deadpan comedic

stare came to full fruition in that moment. And, he said, he thought I should apologize.

I refused. Because it was a joke. A bad one—and also a *great one* that my friends and I still laugh about to this day because we're monsters—but comedy is hard and dying is easy. And I will not make an AIDS joke here, and how dare you for even suggesting it.

THROUGH *QUEERTY* AND, later, other outlets, I was able to engage with the gay community and thus able to feel more a part of it. I developed such a deep knowledge and understanding of LGBTQ+ issues, not just in America but also internationally. Uganda's "Kill the Gays" bill, Russia's anti-gay propaganda, anti-gay purges in Chechnya. It was a fun few years. But it wasn't all doom butt-fucking gloom. I got to report on *Obergefell v. Hodges*, the Supreme Court case that legalized same-sex marriage in America. I got to write about Africa's homophobic roots vis-à-vis its history of colonialism using a healthy supply of GIFs. I got to observe the amazing shift in visibility and acceptance of trans folks. I got to interview *far too many* queens from *RuPaul's Drag Race*.

I thought I was being of service to my community, in however small a capacity. But in return I felt used and abused and discarded by my employer. *Queerty* was based out of San Francisco, so I worked remotely, as did a colleague whose edits somehow often resulted in more errors in my writing than there were to begin with, but I could understand, partially, because he was as burned-out as I was. And had been doing it for longer.

As a writer, I was expected to produce between seven and ten posts a day. I was young and had lucked into becoming a writer, and so I jumped at the chance. They didn't have to be long or involved posts, but often I got carried away. If I was to put my name on something, I had to be proud of it. And more than once at *Queerty* I asked for my name to be removed from a story if I didn't agree with it. I might have been young and inexperienced, but I had a baked-in sense of artistic integrity. Which was why I was broke. That and *Queerty* worked me to the bone and paid me in marrow. The pressure of writing that much, five days a week, and the stress of my finances burned me out completely. And I had a breakdown.

ONLINE MEDIA HAS been on a steady, and at times rapid, decline for . . . about as long as I've been working in it. I've always had excellent timing. Online media presaged the death of print, the most protracted death in history, but a death nonetheless. Smartphones were the final nail in print's coffin, as print continues to beat at its lid, crying out that *it's still alive, dammit, despite popular belief.* Though print media is definitely not long for this earth, online media is experiencing its own demise.

We're living, undeniably, in the most informed age in history. There is so much information, and it is so readily available, and yet people are still out here being ignorant as fuck. Part of the reason is that there's too much information—and too much of it is absolute nonsense. There are also too many sources—and too many of them are nonsense. The very *idea* of truth is up for debate. In this climate, online media sites—whether they be news, entertainment, sports, what have you—emphasize quantity over quality, churning out content, content, content, always, always, always, to grab the wandering attentions of billions of increasingly disinterested peoples.

Conglomerates gobble up websites and brands in order to get a bigger share of ad dollars, yet there always seem to be fewer and fewer ad dollars. This, despite the fact that the proletariat continues to buy things, necessary and otherwise, with its stagnant wages. And then there's the absurd wealth gap of our late-capitalist, early-apocalypse era. Just look at the salaries of the heads of those conglomerates. And then, for a good laugh, look at the salaries of the people churning out the content. I used to make $24,000 at *Queerty*. Writing ten posts a day. A decade and some change later, I make more at *Entertainment Weekly*, but not as much as I'm worth. Or as much as my peers at other outlets, according to industry averages.

In the end, the industry is going down in flames. With the acceleration of artificial intelligence like deepfake videos, the dismantling of facts and reality, and the growing apathy toward all of these things as well as the general fate of the world in which we live, online media isn't going to be able to compete at all. Maybe online will even beat print to the grave.

THAT I WAS making 24K a year writing ten posts a day and living in Brooklyn meant that I eventually got evicted for not paying my rent. This was after I went through two nervous breakdowns at *Queerty*—which did nothing to help me, certainly not in the compensation department. In fact, *Queerty* fired me shortly after that second nervous breakdown. So within a month, I lost my apartment and my job.

Still, it was a relief to be free of that job. While it had given me a sense of gay purpose, it took a toll on my well-being.

For a few months I crashed at a friend's place, collected unemployment, and resuscitated my career through freelancing—which also sucked. At least with a salaried job, I got a regular paycheck, no matter how small. As a freelancer, I found I often had to chase down the money owed to me. The unemployment checks made it possible for me to pursue that particular career angle, because I certainly wasn't getting paid a living wage. All the while, every outlet I wrote for told me how talented a writer I was and how lucky they were to have me. All nice to hear, but talent is not free. It also shouldn't be cheap. Literally anyone can write, but not everyone can write well.

Simply put, talent is not valued in the world of online media. That's why print refuses to die absolutely. There's still a degree of quality, of substance and regard, associated with print that online cannot and will never achieve. Nor does online media care to. It's all about ad dollars, which is revenue. My perspective doesn't matter so much as my ability to churn out content, content, content, always, always, always.

FREELANCING EVENTUALLY GOT me in the door at *Out*, and once I got there, I refused to leave. I had never even heard of *Queerty* when I first started working for them, but of course I knew *Out*. I grew up with *Out*—well, around *Out*. Sneaking around *Out*. Spotting *Out* on magazine racks, tucked away in the "Gay" section, along with the nation's oldest queer mag, *The Advocate*; the fun and flirty *XY*; and the porn. But *Out*, despite its reliance on shirtless white boys on its covers, wasn't porn. Besides toned abs, their covers also featured queer celebrities and allies who might be tackling a gay role in their upcoming film. It was the most mainstream gay publication, and unlike the other mags and sites, their fashion editorials were on point. Not just some thots in underwear and Speedos by daddy's pool. It was all fashion and entertainment with some social issues sprinkled throughout, and I wanted to be a part of it.

The key to success, I've found over the years, is just sticking around. Sure, talent, drive, ambition, connections, and luck all play their part, but sometimes it comes down to just hanging around long enough. It's the same with celebrity. Any star experiencing a downturn in their wattage need only stick around long enough to be appreciated by a new generation with a new way of seeing them. Because we all love a comeback. And I've had tons. After losing my apartment and my job within weeks of each other, I managed to rebound with a job at *Out*, first as a contributor, then as an associate editor, and finally as a senior editor. That took the relatively short time of about three years, mostly because there was so much turnover and upheaval at *Out* and I hung in there long enough to be promoted. While also churning out some good content.

I continued writing my little gay essays about issues affecting me personally, in hopes they would resonate with other fags, and also did the news and pop culture commentary thing, which paid the bills. And the bills were more or less getting paid. Because *Out* and *The Advocate* were owned by the same company, Pride Media, and shared the same tiny office in the Carroll Gardens neighborhood of Brooklyn, their writers often overlapped. During one of the weekly staff meetings, *The Advocate*'s then editor in chief, Matthew Breen, assigned me a piece on the history of Black Gay Pride, the concept and the events surrounding it, for *The Advocate*'s big double Pride issue for June/July.

Print stories were assigned at least two months ahead of publication, so I had time. During that time, what was supposed to be the cover story fell through and *The Advocate* decided to use my story to replace it. It was 2016, and ya gurl had her first magazine cover story. Gay old college dropout me. And for the oldest, most respected gay magazine in all the gay land. And it was about Black shit. The cover featured this beaming Black woman wearing disco ball earrings. I was so proud. For the first time, I was feeling some kind of creative fulfillment. I loved what I was doing, and I was writing for a brand that I respected. It wasn't an Oscar or anything, but it was something.

But when things are going well, I've come to expect the rug to be pulled out from under me at any time. The expectation, the pessimistic anticipation, makes the landing that much easier. *Out*'s editor in chief at the time was the Syrian British, lantern-jawed Aaron Hicklin, who was, it seemed, constantly being pulled in every other direction. But he would always be in the office for the hectic closing of the print issue every month. Once I started working on the print side of *Out* in addition to the web side, I got to know and really like Aaron, and he became the closest thing I've ever had to a mentor. He encouraged my writing and assigned me stories that challenged me as a writer because he knew I could handle them.

My first cover story for *Out* was my piece on *Moonlight*, on its journey from indie darling to top Oscar contender. The mag then flew me out to Los Angeles to interview RuPaul for *Out*'s twenty-fifth-anniversary cover story.

I had interviewed RuPaul once before, over the phone. It didn't start well. I hate doing interviews, especially over the phone, because they make my insecurity around speaking that much more pronounced. Pun unintended. Okay, that's a lie, too, puns are always intended. But I'm not a big "talker." I usually prefer, and cherish, the sound of silence, and I tend to trip over my words when I do have to talk. I get nervous, no matter whom I'm speaking to, and I rush out the words. And I speak so quietly that I anticipate being asked to repeat myself. I'm a failure even before opening my mouth. I just don't have the confidence in the spoken word that I have in the written one. This is all to say: the first RuPaul interview was almost a disaster.

It was about some bullshit reality show, *Skin Wars*, a skin-painting competition between professional makeup artists. I started by asking him what drew him to the show. "A paycheck," he said flatly. I felt my asshole clench in on itself. The last thing you want as an interviewer is that—one- or two-word answers from someone who, it seems, doesn't want to be there. As the interview went on, I got more and more nervous. He kept telling me he couldn't understand me. I got very flustered. But RuPaul, to my surprise, was really patient with me. He could sense that I was having a hard time and told me to just breathe and said that we would start over and just have a regular conversation.

It was better after that. And I even managed to make him laugh. Before we hung up the phone, he had looked me up or something, and of course I was shirtless in the picture he unearthed. He told me, "You've got great tits."

"Thanks," I said. "They cost enough."

And he laughed that big, boisterous RuPaul cackle. That laugh made the entire ordeal worth it. I felt what it must be like to be one of those struggling queens on *Drag Race* who was definitely being eliminated soon but who still felt the warmth of Mama Ru's glow right before getting sent home to an Ariana Grande song.

I doubt Ru remembered that interaction when I went to interview him in Los Angeles, but I came *prepared* this time. I'm talking pages of notes, gurl.

The assignment was to walk through Ru's career, the highs and lows, as his rise coincided with the history of *Out*. He was even one of *Out*'s first cover stars, shot in 1994, at the height of his *Supermodel of the World* phase, by Herb Ritts. We tried to get Ru to shoot a new cover for us for the anniversary issue, but he refused and instead sent over some file glamour shot. We at *Out* all agreed . . . it wasn't the best. As a workaround, we zhuzhed up that file photo and used it as a secondary cover, then broke the bank to get another old Ritts photo—a gorgeous shot starring Ru, gams akimbo—that we all loved. All in all, the twenty-fifth-anniversary issue came out pretty good. But once the magazine's ownership changed hands, as is far too common in media, prompting a mass exodus of staff, including Aaron, I realized that my tenure there had come to an end.

BY THE TIME I left *Out*, I had grown disillusioned with queer media. Compensation for writers and editors across media is, to put it plainly, hot garbage, but it's even worse at under-resourced queer outlets. To further exacerbate matters, having come from poverty and never learning how to not be poor, I was terrible with money. Did you know when you're a 1099 employee, as opposed to a W-2 employee, you have to set aside a portion of your paychecks to pay your taxes at the end of each year since they're not automatically taken out? Well, if you did know that, hooray for fucking you. Meanwhile, I accumulated thousands in unpaid taxes.

The money, or lack thereof, was one thing, but I also felt like I was limiting myself, both in what I could write and in the audience I was able to reach. So often I had worked really hard on a piece only for it to be seen by a few hundred people, if that. I felt I was toiling away in obscurity for little pay.

I was also not a journalist. I had never claimed to be. I was a writer, first and foremost, and a pop culture junkie second. I did my best to report on serious news, but I would quickly tell you: I'm not the gurl for that.

Moreover, I had grown disillusioned with the queer community in general. The two of us never had that strong a connection to begin with. Through queer media I felt I was getting slightly closer to truly loving my community. I just never felt that love back. While I was reporting about the homophobia in Moscow, I was getting called a nigger back at home. The bars and clubs were never my safe space; that was never my community. And any attempt to find community on the apps was foolhardy at best. You can't form community with a torso. Or with a bridge, or a meme, or other apparently viable forms of profile pictures. The internet strips us of our humanity, of the humanity we see in others and ourselves.

The apps didn't replace the bars or make them obsolete, but they did damage the idea of a community. It had less to do with attraction than plain old respect. Saying "no Blacks, no femmes, no fats, no Asians," etc. didn't make me see white faggots as part of my community. Nor did their comments make me feel like a part of theirs. If anything, they were the enemy. Soon a few shitty white gays ruined all white gays for me.

The racial divide between Black and white gays is very real. Left to our own devices, we'd inhabit separate worlds and ne'er the twain shall meet. I've been to white parties—which are just marketed as regular parties, only with overwhelmingly white iconography, like go-go boys—and they're majority white with a few non-white gurls sprinkled in between. I've been to Black parties—which are marketed as such to emphasize the safety (from whiteness) of the safe space—and there are inevitably a few white gurls sprinkled throughout. They're the "acceptable" ones. The ones invited to the proverbial barbecue.

But a space where Black and white gays come together organically? That's rare. Only the most bougie and delusional

Black gays always feel comfortable or welcomed in de facto white gay spaces. The rest of us would sometimes just not bother. They either don't have our music (my queendom for a ratchet turn-up), or their bartenders openly ignore us, or we're just subject to increased scrutiny by security. For how much things have changed for the LGBTQ+ community, the racial divide is still standing firm. Because, well, America.

But that's an observation from someone whose main inter-action with the gays comes from dating apps, which only recently got rid of racial search filters. Grindr can still feel like *Plessy v. Ferguson* happened yesterday. That's not the real world, though. My time for going out in the real, gay world has expired. I may still have a few years left before my sell-by date, but I've more or less retired from the streets. When I *have* gone out, tempted by youthful memories of doing a spread eagle at the Eagle, I'm reminded of how old I am—and not in the "Hi, daddy" way but in the "Isn't it past your bedtime?" way. While I feel out of place and out of time with the younger queers, I've noticed that they actually practice what they preach when it comes to inclusivity. In a way that my generation never did.

Inclusivity of race, gender identity, gender expression, body type. At events, their rainbow flags have the black and brown stripes in solidarity with the QPOC community and the pink, light blue, and white stripes in recognition of the trans, gender-nonconforming, and intersex communities. I mean, the rainbow flag was ugly before, but it's absolutely hideous now. Hideous but intentionally, even aggressively, inclusive. If I weren't so cranky, I might even find a spot for myself.

MY TIME WITH the upcoming legendary children has been brief, as per my intention. I worked with them at *Out*, and I found them mostly obnoxious know-it-alls lacking the range to back it up. I'll concede, however, that I'm a grumpy old faggot, and I have been old way before I even hit puberty. But something about deeming Katy Perry iconic really just rubbed me the wrong way. Violently. I mean, "Teenage Dream" is a great song, but it's fucking Max Goddamn Martin, what the fuck do you expect?

It's crucial to understand the relationship between a gay man and his diva—or divas, as is often the case. A gay's diva is his mother, sister, daughter, best friend, and therapist all in one. So to speak negatively of her is to gain an enemy for life. We've grown real lax with the word, but that's an entirely different essay—one I wrote several years ago. I would never disrespect another gay's diva, but there might at least be a raised eyebrow. Divas, thankfully, are a gay fixation that transcends generations.

These younger fags' kind of gay is a different gay than mine. It's less campy, less stereotypical, less broad, with fewer broads (I worry for the character actresses aging into gay iconhood). Their faggotry is informed by social media, Tumblr, Reddit, memes, GIFs, the whole-ass internet. Their youth was far more openly queer than mine, which reduces the reliance on and thus the importance of subtlety. So much of my kind of gay is snarky comebacks, the mother tongue of every gay and gay-coded character from the twentieth century. I had very few examples of how to be gay, whereas these baby kweens had the gay world, past and present, at their grubby little fingertips.

I'm sure older gays thought the same of the gays in my generation. We were definitely obnoxious know-it-alls. But we at least respected them. Loudly making AIDS jokes directly in front of them notwithstanding. I befriended the gays I did because we all had a similar queer sensibility, the same kind of gay. But our gayness was even out of step with our own generation. My friend Dane and I would often joke that we died on the floor of Studio 54 and got reincarnated in this shithole timeline. Simply put, we were the kinds of gays older gays didn't resent. We kept their memories alive, we worshipped their divas, we quoted their movies, we spoke their language, we knew their history—and without being asked.

The fear of being forgotten. That's why every gay generation hates the next. That, and they don't understand them. They don't understand the hype around their divas, they don't like their clothes, they disagree with their politics and their methods, they resent being replaced by the younger, hotter models, and, most of all, they envy—and, to a degree, resent—their freedom, the freedom that they helped make possible.

I personally didn't do shit. I didn't march, I didn't vote. I wrote some articles, but that's about it. I also don't mind the so-called divas of today. They're not my divas. I couldn't pick most of them out of a vocal lineup. But they're fine. Bops are being had. The less said about this generation's clothes, the better. And that's coming from someone actively wearing Crocs . . . while still side-eyeing other people who are actively wearing Crocs, so, whatever. I also agree with and admire a lot of their politics. I thought you were supposed to get less radical as you got older, but I find the opposite to be true. The more I understand about our capitalist society, the greater my urge is to tear it the fuck down. However, I do find the urge to tear it the fuck down a bit simplistic and think doing so would cause more harm if there's no plan to effectively rebuild that which has been destroyed. Especially when the rebuilding will fall to the still younger and future generations.

Aging as a gay man is a funny thing. I mean, it's definitely giving echoes of *Death in Venice*. Meanwhile, Gustav von Aschenbach, the dude who dies in Venice, is like in his early fifties. That's prime daddy territory. My favorite territory. I was never into younger guys until I started aging into my daddy years. Now I get the hype. But I still tend to gravitate to a daddy. Some gay men just get better as they age, while some peak early and spend their days melting away on a beach chasing after their metaphorical youth. I've always been a late bloomer, so I'm looking forward to getting older, and I am less worried about being replaced by younger, hotter models. Instead, I'm looking forward to scoring the younger, hotter models who, like I was, are into daddies. Aging ain't nothing but opportunity, baby!

Finally, I don't resent or envy the freedoms of this upcoming legendary generation, mostly because I got to experience the acquisition of those freedoms. Therefore I value those freedoms all the more. Coming out was also a pretty painless process for me, but that's in large part due to the sidestepping I did of my family.

Still, I'm not as radical as I'd like to believe. Like a lot of older kweens, I feel some type of way about pronouns and labels.

I WENT TO a few conferences for the NLGJA: The Association of LGBTQ+ Journalists, back when I worked at *Queerty*. That was the first time I recall being asked what my pronouns were. At each conference, we had to go around and say our names, our pronouns, and for whom we wrote. I was rather flippant about the pronouns, because they were never a big deal for me. I understood even then, however, that they were a big deal to some people, and I respected that. After all, what someone chooses to call themselves is none of my business, and abiding by that is not a big fucking deal. Because why not?

Of course, being a cis man, I can afford to be flippant about pronouns because not only am I unlikely to be misgendered, but if I was, it wouldn't mean to me the complete denial of who I am as a person.

I also have my issues with labeling my sexuality. I'm gay, I like dudes, I only like dudes, I'm a Kinsey six-plus. I just . . . really dig dudes. I don't care for men. As a concept and a reality. They're awful. But boy are they pretty. I also use "queer" because I don't always feel like associating myself with other gay men and their stereotypical behavior, notably, their blatant misogyny. It also reflects more of my general outlook on life: queer. I feel similarly about pronouns as I do about labels: I don't care about them for myself, but I'll respect others' decisions to specify them. I hear how some people would prefer no labels at all, which is a great idea in theory, but human beings need to label things in order to understand them. The myriad labels for gender and sexual identities are attempts at fostering understanding.

We just shouldn't conflate understanding and acceptance, nor do I think acceptance is really all that important. When I was reporting on queer issues, I remember switching out "tolerance" for "acceptance," in terms of what we were fighting for as a community. Tolerance was the bare minimum. No, we wanted, we demanded acceptance. But I think fighting for mere acceptance was a folly. Acceptance is unnecessary, and so is understanding. Respect is what it all comes down to, personally. If we can all just respect one another's right to exist, we might stand a chance of salvaging this failing experiment we call the human race.

Acceptance and understanding are nice! They're great; they make everything better. But I think respect has to come first. Otherwise, you may accept and understand me but still try to take away my right to exist.

This younger generation is lucky in how naïve they are. They grew up knowing what it meant to be free, as a lived experience; they grew up knowing they had options, if not necessarily the right, in being who they want to be. They grew up knowing that they exist, that there were others like them, that in some parts of the world that was okay, even celebrated. They grew up more confident in their right to be alive, and with that knowledge engrained in them, they're unlikely to relinquish their rights without a fight. And these kids can organize a protest in front of your house, your mama's house, and your job, all at the same time, in like five minutes.

I guess the only real gripe I have with the younger gays is their goddamn sincerity. Birthed as I was in a cesspool of gay cynicism, the earnestness of this younger generation is jarring. That's in part where all this overreliance on labels and pronouns comes from, the need to be sensitive to other people's identities. It's commendable, really. Just . . . annoying. It feels a bit like micromanaging personal freedom. And sometimes that leads to missing the forest for the trees when it comes to their selective outrage.

Like, there's so much to be angry about when it comes to life in America, and for the sake of what's remaining of my sanity, I won't go into everything, but those problems can seem so big and unsolvable that it's easier to focus on, say, a brand's insensitive ad campaign, because that's something that can be figured out relatively easily and quickly. But the energy spent on policing social media or Corporate America could instead be spent on burning Corporate America to the ground for destroying the world's climate, for hoarding mind-boggling amounts of wealth, for exploiting the labor class to within an inch of its life, etc., etc., etc. Again, I won't go further for the sake of what remains of my sanity. Hint: it's not a lot!

I can't, and I sincerely do not want to, tell anyone how to fight for their rights, especially if I'm usually getting high on the sidelines. But as a stoned casual observer, I find it hard not to notice how conservatives thrive by tripping up their liberal nemeses in so-called identity politics, while liberals rely on those very identity politics to win elections and to absolve themselves of failing those who got them elected in the first place because at least the big tent's got you covered. The gays are an easy target, the transgender community even more so. Targeting vulnerable populations in order to avoid dealing with planet- and future-destroying issues like late capitalism and the wealth gap is like the third lesson they teach in political science. Right behind "Greed is good" and "Always be closing . . . the democratic process to as many people as possible."

The thing is, the gays these days . . . are not so easy to please. The gays have actually never been easy. We're a real ornery bunch and can get shit done when we're not fighting or dehumanizing one another. I've witnessed firsthand the pendulum swing from one extreme to the other and seemingly back in this country when it comes to LGBTQ+ rights. I've learned my history, goddammit. I know how the gays have survived and know how the gays will continue to survive, to fight. I do worry sometimes that my constant, reliable criticism of the gays, from my days at *Queerty* to *Out* to this book, does more to harm than help the community. When under attack from the Supreme Court or state assemblies or the president, am I also just micromanaging personal freedom? Am I missing the forest for the trees when the forest is reborn fascism?

I mean, maybe? But also, shut up. The true crux of freedom is that no one's free if we're not all free. If Black people are marginalized within the queer community, then how can we all fight as a united front against the relentless tyranny of twenty-first-century conservatism? Everyone knows the straights are lame, but the gays should be better than that, should be better than racism, or misogyny, or transphobia among our own ranks. That's all I've been trying to tell these stupid faggots all along. God bless 'em. We're better than this.

I HATE THE GAYS

I think the younger gays get it. They're more aware. About everything. Race. Gender. Class. The things that keep us from being free. And knowing them, they're going to label the hell out of all of it. But the good side of labels is, once you name an evil, you get that much closer to destroying it. Because you know what you're fighting. So as much as I don't relate to, or even like, this younger generation of gays, fuck do I respect those faggots.

I have to, as they're really the only hope I have left for this world.

7

VICTIM OR VILLAIN?

IN 1961, CLOSETED British actor Dirk Bogarde starred in *Victim*, one of the first films to deal explicitly and sympathetically with homosexuality, directed by Basil Dearden. Bogarde starred as married barrister Melville Farr, whose picturesque life is upended when he's blackmailed over his homosexual relationship with Jack "Boy" Barrett (portrayed by Peter McEnery), working-class trade who hangs himself to avoid his secret coming out. Farr avoids such a grim fate, only having his life ruined.

Before this film, most gay, or rather, queer-coded, characters were the villains. Mrs. Danvers in *Rebecca*, Dracula's daughter of that titular film, Waldo Lydecker and his acid tongue in *Laura*, Addison DeWitt and his acid tongue in *All About Eve*, the gays at the center of Alfred Hitchcock's *Rope*, and perhaps the most famous example, Hitchcock's Norman Bates from *Psycho*, which came out just a year before *Victim*.

But those characters' sexualities were never discussed. It was as if finally mentioning homosexuality elicited not sympathy, but some kind of pity. Pity for those poor gay bastards.

Most queer stories since have painted their characters as victims. Victims of society, of their own twisted psychology, victims of violence or murder. And, in reality, queer people have largely been victims, targets of hysteria, scapegoats of despots, among the most vulnerable of populations. When Trump was elected in 2016, he ushered in a new wave of attacks on the LGBTQ+ community, rolling back protections set in place by the Obama administration. Most of those protections had been made through executive order, as the forty-fourth president infamously lacked any congressional support in his second term, thus rendering them tenuous at best for future presidencies.

Queer people were afraid all over again, having found some semblance of safety amid the progress of the previous eight years. Aside from marriage equality, queer people could find comfort in knowing they had an ally in the White House. Obama appeared on the cover of *Out* in 2015, the first and only president to do so. Trump would receive no such invitation.

Trump and his cronies went after LGBTQ+ rights with clear-eyed focus—a focus notably lacking in nearly every other corner of his administration. He banned trans military service members from the armed forces; appointed a spate of anti-LGBTQ+ judges across the judicial system, from local courts to the Supreme Court; stripped Obama policies protecting trans and nonbinary workers against employment discrimination; and weaponized Title IX against trans students, among a series of other actions. In a harbinger of what his presidency would become, within hours of Trump being sworn in, information on LGBTQ+ rights on government websites was completely eliminated. Trump also sparked a revival of open white supremacy in this country, bringing khaki-and-polo-wearing fascists out into the daylight.

And into this powder keg Jussie Smollett threw a flaming match. In January 2019, I was working at Logo, the queer cable network that had originally given us *RuPaul's Drag Race* when it was still produced on a shoestring budget with camera lenses swathed in Vaseline. I wrote for their news and pop culture website, NewNowNext, with some occasional crossover into the cable territory. Near the end of the month, Smollett made headlines as the victim, so he claimed, of an attack by MAGA extremists.

Smollett was an openly gay actor on Lee Daniels's primetime soap opera, *Empire*, where he played openly gay musician Jamal Lyon. While loved unconditionally by his mother, Jamal frequently contended against his father's and the music industry's homophobia. The actor was also a member of the Smollett family of actors, including his younger, more talented sister Jurnee. Smollett claimed he had been approached late at night in Chicago by two men wearing masks, who asked him, "Aren't you that faggot *Empire* nigger?" He said they then tied a noose around his neck, poured bleach on him, and yelled, "MAGA country!"

Looking back on it, the story does seem . . . far-fetched, embellished by trace notes of actorly melodrama. Smollett had previously claimed he had received a threatening letter in the mail with the words "You will die Black faggot" rendered in cutout letters. Like, who does that outside of the cartoonish villains in 1960s *Batman* TV episodes?

But this was, after all, MAGA country. Hate crimes under Trump increased by nearly 20 percent from the Obama years. White supremacists were marching the streets, unhooded, carrying tiki torches and yelling about how they wouldn't be "replaced." We were living in far-fetched times, and Smollett's alleged attack seemed like just another logical step into the abyss of daily life that had marked the forty-fifth president's chaotic tenure.

As I was the first writer to report on the Smollett news for NewNowNext, and as I was the only Black writer on staff, I was assigned the Jussie Smollett beat. I would follow and report on all the developments. At first, I accepted the beat out of some vague sense of duty, as the only Black writer on staff. It was my duty, I felt, as a queer person of color to report on this story for other queer people of color, as evidence of the very real dangers we faced.

Soon, the messages of support started flooding in from celebrities, including Daniels and *Empire*'s undeniable star, Taraji P. Henson, who portrayed Jamal's fiercely loyal mother, Cookie Lyon. Smollett's family released a statement on his behalf, affirming that his story had "never changed" and making sure to note that "these targeted hate crimes are happening to our sisters, brothers, and our gender non-conforming siblings" all across the country. Fox Entertainment and 20th Century Fox Television, *Empire*'s parent companies, pledged their love for Smollett, vowing to work with law enforcement to "bring these perpetrators to justice."

The next day, I saddled up my high horse and wrote an essay on Smollett's attack, "The Audacity to Be Young, Black, and Gay." I started by referencing Montgomery, Alabama's Equal Justice Initiative opening the first-ever museum and memorial honoring the 4,084 victims of what it terms "racist terror lynchings" in 2018.

Far from reparations, the Legacy Museum and the National Memorial for Peace and Justice represented one of the few times America had dared to grapple with its shameful history of racial terrorism. And yet, it seemed, here it was—still happening. Senator Cory Booker and future vice president Kamala Harris initially called the attack on Smollett "an attempted modern-day lynching."

Jamal Lyon, Smollett's character on *Empire*, was groundbreaking at the time, the bar for Black queer characters being relatively low. He was openly gay, had no angst about it, and had a good relationship with most of his family, save his homophobic father, Terrence Howard's Lucious Lyon. Jamal was a beacon for Black queer representation, and Smollett became that, too.

"Like Jamal, Smollett has striven to be an outspoken advocate for the Black and queer communities and has lived his life publicly, openly, and without shame," I wrote, continuing:

It's 2019 and we still have to deal with unchecked racial hate, but far from being intimidated or broken, I am enraged. I can only hope that Jussie Smollett has the love and support he needs to continue living his life publicly, openly, and without shame—that he remains audaciously young, Black, and gay. What happened to him shouldn't happen to anyone; that it happened to him, a famous person with means and a platform, is important to continue this discussion on a national level, but what of the Black men whose lives become a footnote in the seemingly endless collection of police shootings, or the Black trans women forced into victimhood by the sole merit of their existence?

I was so goddamn earnest. But this, I thought, was why I got into queer journalism in the first place. To be able to say something of substance that benefits my community. And I was inspired to do more. I brought an idea to my editor Matthew Breen, who had given me my first cover story when he was still running *The Advocate*, though had since moved on to Logo. With access to the latter's production capabilities, I decided to go the extra step, to actually do something about my rage, and produce a roundtable discussion with Black queer activists, tackling the Smollett incident and the general threat of hate crimes afflicting our community.

With the help of the rest of the news team, I put together a panel that included Emil Wilbekin, the former editor in chief of *Vibe* magazine and founder of Native Son, an advocacy group for Black queer men. I had always looked up to Emil as an openly gay Black man and was familiar with him through his work at *Vibe* and as a talking head on VH1's endless collection of pop culture retrospective shows. I finally got to meet him when I interviewed him about Native Son for *Out*. He was the first person I thought of to join this roundtable, and he accepted my invitation without hesitation.

I had never produced anything like this before, with real camera operators and sets and craft services. I was so pleased with myself. *I could even win a GLAAD Award for this*, I thought privately, and rather selfishly. I don't do things for awards, but I still like them, and I have never won anything in my adult life. This was my chance to finally get acknowledged for my work by my community, as I had been working as a queer journalist for the better part of a decade and had never gotten so much as an honorable mention. A timely discussion on this shocking incident that galvanized so many issues currently at play in American life? Pass the envelope!

Our video went live on February 6, playing online and on the Logo channel. Ten days later, Smollett's story started to unravel. There had already been rumors that the attack had been a hoax, a publicity stunt by Smollett over anxiety his *Empire* character was being written off the show. I dismissed those rumors. Who—*who?!* I ask you—would possibly stage an attack, preying on an already sensitive and precarious sociopolitical climate to further some personal agenda? I know we as a society love to diagnose sociopathy sans credentials with the ease of a flippant remark, but that sounded like true sociopathic behavior.

But again, we were living in far-fetched times. And if Smollett's attack story was far-fetched, what actually happened, insofar as we know what actually happened, was just plain bonkers. Days after the attack, Smollett reemerged, phoenixlike, to perform at a previously scheduled concert in West Hollywood. "The most important thing that I can say is to keep it simple and say thank you and I'm okay," Smollett told the cheering, sold-out crowd, which included *Empire* co-creator Lee Daniels and Congresswoman Maxine "Reclaiming My Time" Waters. "I'm not fully healed yet, but I'm going to, and I'm going to stand strong with you all."

I had friends who went to that show in support of Smollett. "I had to be here tonight," the actor continued. "I couldn't let those motherfuckers win!"

There had already been some issues with the inconsistencies of his story, but Smollett brushed them aside to the adoring crowd. We ran the story with a photo of Smollett, backlit, appearing Christlike in a white shirt, reaching out his benevolent hand to an audience member. "During times of trauma, grief, and pain, there is still a responsibility to lead with love," he had said two days earlier in his first official statement. "It's all I know. And that can't be kicked out of me."

Now, addressing his adoring crowd, he told them that the most important thing was that he "fought the fuck back!," eliciting cheers from the audience. "I'm the gay Tupac!" he added, I thought (and hoped) at the time, jokingly. But I should've known this nigga was on one as soon as he said that.

Two weeks later, Smollett's alleged attackers were released from custody without being charged. They were identified as two jacked Nigerian brothers, who, it seemed, had known Smollett before the attack. The day before, Smollett's first televised interview aired on *Good Morning America*. He "broke his silence" with Robin Roberts, sticking by his story, which was sounding more and more implausible. But the deeper he got into it all, the more he dug his heels in, delivering a teary performance defending his dwindling credibility.

"I'm an advocate," he told Roberts. "I respect too much the people—who I am now one of those people—who have been attacked in any way. You do such a disservice when you lie about things like this."

But then the police called Smollett's bluff. With the release of his alleged attackers, the Chicago Police Department suggested that Smollett had orchestrated the attack. Smollett had hired one of the brothers as his personal trainer and followed them both on Instagram. One of them had even appeared as an extra on *Empire*. Once the lies started adding up, the brothers sang like canaries. By this point I wanted nothing to do with the Smollett beat. But I didn't have much choice in the matter.

I called the next essay I wrote on Smollett the very direct "What the Actual F*ck Is Going on Here?" This whole shit show made me so nervous for a number of reasons. There was the fear of the MAGA acolytes being vindicated as the victims they saw themselves as, despite their actions having created a climate in which an attack like the one Smollett had devised could plausibly happen. There was the fear of liberals being wrong in their righteous indignation, which was all they clung to in the dark ages of Trump. And there was the fear of how these shenanigans might affect future victims of assault.

"I can't help but feel . . . not betrayed, that's not the word," I wrote. "Maybe naïve . . . and more than a little disillusioned. Not by Smollett himself, but the circumstances surrounding him." In time, "betrayed" would be the word. Betrayed by

Jussie Smollett, mostly. The actor was charged with a felony count of disorderly conduct for filing a false police report.

The Chicago PD claimed Smollett faked a threatening letter, then a week later paid the two brothers $3,500 to stage an attack because he was "dissatisfied with his salary" on *Empire*. They said they even had the check Smollett used in the transaction.

A check?!

Not even a Cash App? A Venmo? A Zelle? Just plain cash? No, instead he uses the most traceable form of payment. All those years of acting and he never learned you don't leave a fucking paper trail? That's literally how every villain gets caught. But Jussie Smollett didn't think of himself as the villain. He was the victim here. He continued to maintain his innocence, even when all evidence pointed to the contrary.

It wasn't long before Smollett became an official object of national ridicule and resentment, when *Saturday Night Live* parodied him shortly after he was charged. Cast member Chris Redd played Smollett in a *Shark Tank* parody, *Shark Tank: Legal Edition*, in which the sharks are embattled lawyers. When Smollett is asked why he's there, he simply responds, "I broke humanity."

That felt about right. This was outrageous! This was some shit that would've happened on *Empire*, where ridiculous people did ridiculous things all the time. Perhaps Smollett got reality and television confused, sort of like *A Double Life* but super dumb. In that 1947 film directed by the great and gay George Cukor, Ronald Colman starred as an actor who gets lost in his character, Shakespeare's Othello, as the lines between the play and his real life gradually disappear altogether.

It's definitely giving too much credit to Smollett's acting chops that he would go so deep into Jamal Lyon to come out thinking a scheme of soap-operatic proportions would actually work. Aside from the obvious paper trail, there were so many lazy missteps and miscalculations. He had staged the attack hoping it would get caught on a security camera, but the camera was pointing the wrong way and missed all the action. Actors always wanna be directors, but some of them can't quite cut the mustard.

The assailants Smollett had paid to attack him *were* caught on camera, however—buying the gloves, ski masks, and red hat that they used in the attack. Also, those two dudes were Black as night. African Black. Smollett couldn't find some dumb white guys to pull this off, to at least give the attack some semblance of verisimilitude?

I love heist movies. It's fantastic when a plan comes together and the criminals walk away with all the goods. And you root for the criminals; they're the heroes in this situation. But it's also equally entertaining when the plan goes terribly awry and the criminals are hoisted by their own petards. And Smollett's petard was hoisted all over the place. Though the initial charges against him were dropped in March 2019, in exchange for community service and a $10,000 bond, the following month the city of Chicago sued Smollett for the $130,000 it had wasted on the investigation, no doubt utilizing resources that could have gone to a legitimate hate crime. Months later, in November,

Smollett had the gall, the unmitigated cheek, to countersue the city, alleging he was the victim of "mass public ridicule and harm."

But whose fault was that, sis? For minority groups in America, victimhood is a natural state, one in which you feel you are constantly under attack by the white majority and the apparatuses they use to remain in power: the government, law enforcement, etc., etc. The white majority, in turn, loves to blame victims for their own victimhood, rather than empathizing with the conditions that continue to marginalize groups. And under Trump, white people were free to play the victims, too. Whiteness was under attack, and it was the right of every white person in America to defend themselves against this attack, by any means necessary.

What a crock of shit. Apparently by 2045, white people will cease to be the majority in America. That's not because they're under attack; it's because the world is changing. Races intermarry, immigration persists at a steady clip, and white folks just aren't popping out babies like they used to. Whiteness is not the victim here. But then you have someone like Jussie Smollett who gives credence to fragile white arguments.

The legal case against Smollett dragged on for years. In 2022, he was sentenced to 150 days in prison, and during his hearing, he turned the courtroom into a one-man show, repeatedly shouting that he was "not suicidal," on the off chance he somehow ended up dead in his cell. Okay, Epstein. The presiding judge repeatedly called Smollett "narcissistic, selfish, and arrogant." He ended up serving six days of his sentence. His *Empire* character, however, was, in a deliciously ironic twist, written off the show, the fate he had allegedly been trying to avoid. *Empire* was canceled the following season, mostly due to low ratings, but the Smollett controversy didn't help matters. Or those ratings.

Smollett continued to deny being the absolute worst, though his demeanor through this whole ordeal certainly precluded that. In a podcast interview a month after he was released from prison, he said he would never have concocted a hate crime hoax because that would "mean that I stuck my fist in the pain of Black Americans in this country for over four hundred years" and "stuck my fist in the fears of the LGBTQ community all over the world. I'm not that motherfucker—never have been, don't need to be."

Just because someone is Black doesn't mean they can't intentionally harm the Black community. Clarence Thomas has made a career of it. That Uncle Tom in judicial robes. And so has conservative pundit Candace Owens. And Kanye West, for that matter. They use their own pretzel logic, like Smollett has done, to defend their actions, but Black folks don't buy their shit and they're never invited to the cookout. Smollett's pass, too, has permanently been revoked. And as seen with the Gays for Trump, gay people aren't above selling out their own people either.

The 2021 film *Judas and the Black Messiah* highlighted one of modern history's great Black betrayers, FBI informant William O'Neal, who insinuated himself into the inner circle of Chicago's Black Panther Party, leading to the assassination of the charismatic leader Fred Hampton. Hampton galvanized support among Chicago's disenfranchised communities, across races, forming the Rainbow Coalition to include the Panthers, the poor whites of the Young Patriots, and the Hispanics of the Young Lords. Like Huey Newton, Hampton understood the need to unite the masses against a threat that affected them all. And so, like Huey Newton, he had to be eliminated.

After his betrayal, O'Neal lived under the witness protection program for fifteen years and finally told his story in the 1989 documentary series *Eyes on the Prize*. The night his episode aired, O'Neal died by suicide.

How does it feel to betray one's own people? To "stick a fist" in their pain? I don't know for sure if Smollett orchestrated his hate crime, though I'm strongly inclined to agree that he did, but I can imagine that the immense guilt from doing something so objectively terrible would break someone's mind. Smollett might have to believe he is innocent; otherwise he wouldn't be able to live with himself. Every interview I've seen with him is of a person divorced from reality.

In all fairness, though—reality does suck. Smollett and I are about the same age, both Black, both gay, both with maternal affection for Taraji P. Henson. I can understand the urge to, really, burn all this to the goddamn ground. Smollett simply weaponized his identity. And had he gotten away with it, no thanks to that meddling Chicago PD, he would've been . . . not the gay Tupac but at least the gay Drake. An endearing, if at times questionable, light-skinned nigga.

While I could easily argue that Smollett's relative wealth and notoriety inoculated him against the worst intentions of this country, he was never wealthy or famous enough to be completely immune to the twin diseases of racism and homophobia.

I can say that for someone without his means and privilege, the constant pressures of being marginalized, demonized, and scapegoated can drive you mad.

When you've been victimized all your life—by society, by family, by your own insecurities forged from a life of hardship—you tend to see victimization everywhere, whether it exists or not. And you can either succumb to that victimization or find a way to make it work for you. For instance: White guilt. The gift that keeps on giving. No person of color should ever give up the opportunity to capitalize on white guilt. It's our birthright. Your ancestors enslaved my ancestors? Affirmative action should be the least you can do.

But it is maddening, to be a minority within a minority. You can start to think you deserve to be punished, to struggle, to be unhappy; you begin to think you are less than, that you are unworthy. And when you feel unworthy, that your life will always be impossibly hard, what's to stop you from just saying, "Fuck it," and burning it all to the ground? The victim becomes the villain. If you're taught to believe that you're the villain, the cause of all society's ills, then you might relent and embody the villain. It's what inner-city Black kids have been dealing with for generations. But Smollett is not an inner-city kid.

I have no interest in or intention of explaining or justifying Smollett's motivations, but he capitalized on very real injustices that were all too easy to believe. If he did what it's pretty evident he did, then he sold out both Black and queer people for personal gain and salvation. He weaponized victimization and in doing so became a villain.

HISTORY, MUCH LIKE Disney, is full of gay villains. Unlike Disney, history's gay villains are usually no fun. And certainly not nearly as fabulous as, say, Ursula, the sea witch from *The Little Mermaid*, or Maleficent, the witch queen from *Sleeping Beauty*. Milo Yiannopoulos may have tried to pull off a dramatic cape in his time, but I assure you: It didn't work, mama.

I've always been intrigued by the idea of gay villains, though. Because gays throughout history have been maligned and victimized, we were powerless, and so a gay villain, in my mind, was simply reclaiming the power stripped from them. But what was the price of that power? And was it ever worth it?

Three gay villains come to mind, at least when it comes to the promulgation of white supremacy, which, for my money, is the greatest evil in the world today. The aforementioned Yiannopoulos and his goose-stepping foregays, Renaud Camus and Ernst Röhm.

In 2016, *Out* decided to run a long profile on gay cartoon villain Milo Yiannopoulos, including a photo shoot with that messy faggot dressed up as a clown, as if to make light of his overtly racist and fascist rhetoric. It was a terrible idea, which much of the staff told editor in chief Aaron Hicklin. But Aaron, a real stickler for objective journalism, was blinded by his own commitment to objectivity. Yiannopoulos was gay and making a name for himself in the public sphere, so we, as a gay outlet, had an obligation to cover him. But the photo shoot? That was glamorizing an idiot.

The backlash was swift. The gays called out *Out* for giving

Yiannopoulos a platform, while I and several members of the staff publicly denounced the story. While I can respect Aaron's intentions, there's a right way of dealing with fascists, and dressing them up as Punchinella isn't it.

Yiannopoulos was another in a disturbing line of white faggots who cozied up to, and enabled, fascism. In 1979, French writer and academic Renaud Camus published *Tricks*, "a sexual odyssey" detailing a young gay Frenchman's twenty-five brief sexual encounters from Paris and the French Riviera to Milan, New York, and San Francisco. Noted literary queer Allen Ginsberg called Camus's world "completely that of a new urban homosexual; at ease in half a dozen countries."

Out of his dozens and dozens of books, *Tricks* remains Camus's most translated work, but he is most famous, or infamous, for the book he published more than thirty years later, which has been widely adopted by white supremacists.

Published in 2012, *Le Grand Remplacement* posits the conspiracy theory that Europe's white majority is in danger of being replaced by Muslim and darker-skinned immigrants from North and sub-Saharan Africa. "The great replacement is very simple," Camus said of his doctrine. "You have one people, and in the space of a generation you have a different people."

The great replacement soon became the raison d'être for white supremacists: In 2019, the New Zealand Christchurch mosque shooter named his manifesto after Camus's book. Before that, angry, tiki torch–wielding white nationalists chanted, "Jews will not replace us!" in Charlottesville, Virginia, during a Unite the Right rally in 2017, which resulted in the death of

Heather Heyer. White supremacy is now the most dangerous and insidious form of terrorism, with considerable thanks to three gay white men.

That Camus once advocated for open borders, at least when it came to the sexual tourism of the modern gay man, and he now desires a xenophobic, ethnically pure France may come as a surprise. But he's hardly the first, or last, homosexual to willfully become an instrument in the spread of white supremacy.

When reached by *The Washington Post* for comment in the wake of the Christchurch massacre, Camus claimed he condemned violence, but at the same time he supported how his conspiracy theory has been interpreted. That same theory has and will continue to lead to increased violence in the name of some alleged "white genocide."

Now. When one thinks of "white genocide," it's usually white people committing genocide against another group, because, well, *facts*. White people are not endangered. The biggest killer of white people is probably other white people. But when it comes to committing genocide, the whites are undefeated.

There was the genocide of indigenous peoples of America by white colonizers, the genocide of Black people in the Jim Crow South by the Ku Klux Klan, and of course the genocide of Jews in Nazi Germany by the ultimate white supremacists, which was also helped along by—you guessed it—a white gay.

AFTER SERVING IN World War I, Ernst Röhm became one of the earliest defectors to the Nazi Party, where he became close friends and political allies with Adolf Hitler. Their friendship has often stoked rumors that Hitler himself was gay.

Initially founded to counter communism in postwar Germany, the Nazi Party rose to power in the early 1920s using an agenda bolstered by pseudoscience and propaganda around the idea of a German master race. In order to achieve racial purity, the party began systematically targeting "inferior" races, most notoriously Jews.

Hitler assumed leadership of the party in 1921, and after he was briefly imprisoned in 1923, he appointed Röhm to take charge of the SA, the Nazi's militia. In 1925, Hitler and Röhm had a falling-out that prompted the latter to find self-imposed exile in Bolivia. Then, in 1930, Hitler telephoned Röhm to tell him that he needed him back in Germany to serve as the SA chief of staff.

Under Röhm, the SA grew into a feared and powerful presence, facilitating the growth of the Nazi Party. Still, the homosexuality of Röhm and other SA officers, including his deputy Edmund Heines, remained a liability to the party—a Socialist Democratic newspaper published a letter from Röhm to a friend spilling the tea on his gay affairs in 1931. Though Hitler was aware of Röhm's sexuality, he didn't seem to have a problem as long as the SA was strong-arming him into power.

Röhm was among the more radical in the Nazi Party leadership, and soon rumbles began that he was a threat to Hitler's power. The SA, with its more than three million members, was unruly and unpredictable, and the moral character of Röhm and others within its ranks (read: the gay thing) led to dissent. Hitler tried to weaken the militia and reduce its numbers, but

Röhm objected. Party conservatives, no fan of "the gay thing," worried more about his political aspirations and feared he would eventually attempt a coup against Hitler. Threatened with martial law and the loss of power, Hitler finally decided to oust Röhm.

On June 30, 1934, Hitler and his SS, the group that had effectively replaced the SA, arrived at the Hanselbauer Hotel near Munich, where Röhm and his supporters were staying. Hitler's forces surprised the sleeping men in a purge known as the Night of the Long Knives. Heines, Röhm's deputy, was caught in bed with an unidentified eighteen-year-old boy; they were both taken outside and shot.

Hitler, still hesitant to send Röhm off to execution, had him arrested and afforded him the opportunity to die by suicide instead. When two senior Nazi officers handed the SA leader a loaded pistol and gave him ten minutes to do the deed, he refused, saying, "If I am to be killed, let Adolf do it himself."

I wonder if Röhm always knew it would end like this. If he guessed that his proximity to power would not ultimately protect him when others were sent to concentration camps for the same sin against nature. I doubt it. But proximity to power is not power itself. And once you become a threat to that power, your days are numbered and whatever deficiencies or abnormalities you possess *will* be used against you. The Nazis were, after all, about purity, and as much as I love it, there's nothing pure about butt sex. That's kinda the appeal.

The officers shot Röhm, and the Nazis attempted to expunge him from its official history, along with the thousands of homosexual men and millions of Jews they imprisoned and killed in concentration camps out of some baseless idea of racial purity. Röhm, however, would prove an inspiration—and yet, somehow, not a warning—for the gay man credited with the twenty-first century's alt-right movement.

PROGRESS IN QUEER rights has never been propelled by cis white men because they can always rely on their identity to buffer them against the myriad injustices of a society initially designed in their favor. Unlike trans people or people of color, they can easily pass within the upper echelons of society's power structures. Key word being "easily." Just look at evil gay billionaire Peter Thiel. Don't look too long or hard or he might sue you, as he did when *Gawker* ran a series of stories effectively outing him in 2007 and he sued the outlet out of existence.

Thiel enacted the kind of revenge I can only dream of, a long game involving Hulk Hogan and years and millions of dollars in lawsuits, ending with *Gawker*'s demise. While the politics of outing people are up for debate, Thiel's proven himself a cozy bedfellow with white supremacists in the past, having met with noted white nationalist Kevin DeAnna in 2016, the same year he emerged as one of Donald Trump's biggest donors. Imagine if the fight for queer visibility were up to the Peter Thiels of the world, men who would gain the whole straight world for the price of their gay soul.

But thankfully we had the Marsha P. Johnsons and Sylvia Riveras of the world, people who couldn't and wouldn't hide in plain sight, and who didn't believe that they should have to either. Some white men would rather align themselves with whiteness, with the status quo, than with what could be perceived as the greater good for what they don't perceive as their own community.

Within a series of emails *BuzzFeed* obtained in its lengthy 2017 exposé on the mainstreaming of the white nationalist movement, Milo Yiannopoulos—then tech editor of the far-right troll factory Breitbart—shared his password with a colleague: "LongKnives1290." The Long Knives in reference to the purge that killed the undesirable Nazis, 1290 referring to the year King Edward I expelled the Jews from England. Yiannopoulos and Breitbart had often and vehemently, amid the threat of litigation, denied that he was a racist or a white nationalist. With the exposé, however, that cover, tenuous at best, was blown.

For several years, Yiannopoulos—emboldened and groomed by Breitbart co-founder Steve Bannon—had played a coy game of First Amendment tag with the media, making vile comments about Muslims, women, gays, and basically anyone he hoped to get a rise out of, while blithely defending his freedom of speech and coating his act in the unconvincing veneer of satire. He built a large following online, frequently testing the limits of Twitter before he was permanently banned in July 2016.

By then, Yiannopoulos had proven himself a useful recruitment tool to the alt-right ideology, his article "An Establishment Conservative's Guide to the Alt-Right" serving as a *Le Grand Remplacement* for bros. As a gay man spouting white nationalist rhetoric, he positioned himself as some sort of chimerical neo-Nazi mascot, like if Ernst Röhm had a bad dye job and a Twitter account. Yiannopoulos took his sadistic show on the road with the Dangerous Faggot tour, darkening the doorsteps of campuses around the United States and United Kingdom. Everywhere he went, Yiannopoulos was greeted by protest, which was entirely the point. He successfully whipped up controversy, and the Breitbart brand only got stronger, Yiannopoulos becoming its polarizing star.

With Breitbart, Yiannopoulos and Bannon tapped into a lingering resentment over the politically correct, inclusive, "love is love" Obama era and weaponized it into a movement encompassing the greatest hits of white male grievance, from anarchism all the way down to xenophobia. The "Jews will not replace us" folks. The Blue Lives Matter, men's rights, white genocide folks. And, most tellingly, the "Make America Great Again" folks. With the election of Donald Trump, the alt-right went from being an online menace to a political and social force to be reckoned with, but Yiannopoulos soon found himself on the outs.

According to the emails *BuzzFeed* retrieved, Yiannopoulos had some lingering resentment over not being able to pontificate at the Republican National Convention in July 2016—an opportunity afforded to noted evil gay billionaire Peter Thiel. "No gays rule doesn't apply to Thiel apparently," he complained. Ironic, isn't it, how people like Röhm, Heines, and Yiannopoulos can actively participate in a group that despises who they are, blatantly uses them to justify its own ends, and just as blatantly discards them once they've outlived their purpose? No, "ironic" isn't the word for it—"sad," "pathetic," "insane." One of those seems more fitting.

For Yiannopoulos, the beginning of the end came when he made some favorable comments about pedophilia in January 2016 that came back to haunt him a year later as he was readying to speak at the Conservative Political Action Conference—where the "gay" rules were apparently a bit more lenient. Yiannopoulos was sabotaged by—surprise, surprise—a conservative website, which unearthed the damning interview, and within days he had been forced to resign from Breitbart. At least publicly. He would lurk about in the shadows, gradually fading into the Breitbart ether as 2017 wore on and he became even more of a caricature of himself.

In his wake, Yiannopoulos left the alt-right—this ginned-up section of American life that dresses white supremacy in respectability and academia, like that of Renaud Camus. But just what they believe in and just what they're so angry about can be confusing, to say the least.

EQUALLY CONFOUNDING: GAYS for Trump. They're no Ernst Röhms or Edmund Heineses or Milo Yiannopoulai, but they do have something in common. It's not self-loathing, which people often attribute to those who seem to go against their own interests. Rather, I think, it's just selfishness. It's putting oneself above all else, even when it's to the detriment of others, of millions, or more. It's seeing one's humanity as greater and more important than someone else's. It has nothing to do with white supremacy; it's a general sense of supremacy, and the belief in one's whiteness is either the scapegoat or the catalyst.

And out of that belief, they lay their chips with the winning hand—the one that's had its thumb on the scale all these centuries. It can be as simple as supporting Trump after getting snubbed by Hillary—as one gay political power couple actually did when Clinton refused a photo with them. Or going all-in at Breitbart because someone terrible believed you were terrible, too. Or railing against the passage of time as some form of white genocide. Or just everything Ernst Röhm did. Though they may claim some higher purpose, that purpose is always self-aggrandizing, at all costs.

WHILE JUSSIE SMOLLETT'S transgressions were hardly on a massive scale, his motive was still self-aggrandizement. I have more sympathy for him than, say, Milo Yiannopoulos, because he's Black. America is built against Black people, so I can understand wanting to even the scales somehow.

What I can't understand is why it was done so badly. I have the same problem with a lot of Black-owned businesses. Like, I want to support them, but there's always something janky going on. There are misspellings on the website, or someone drops the ball on a shipment, or the quality of the product is just not quite there. These shortcomings are usually the product of limited resources and not necessarily incompetence, though with Smollett I think it was just plain incompetence. The resources were there!

If he wanted to pull off a proper scheme, he should've outsourced his deviousness rather than taking it all on himself. Typical rookie mistake. You can't tell me there's not a real-life

Olivia Pope ready and willing to orchestrate a fake hate crime for the right price. If there isn't, that means there's a gaping hole in the market and I'm the swing-coat-wearing diva to do it, dammit. I've fancied myself a villain most of my life anyway. I'm always literally one minor transgression away from resolving to ruin someone's life at all costs.

Belief in my own villainy comes from a rejection of my own victimhood. I hate feeling victimized. I hate feeling helpless. And that hate quickly turns to rage. Maybe it's the Scorpio in me. We're a notoriously vengeful sign. Obsessively vengeful, really. A guy blocked me on Instagram (and Scruff, and Grindr, and probably LinkedIn) months ago and I'm still casually plotting his downfall—and I will continue to as long as I draw breath. Astrology permitting, my instinctive reaction to being hurt is to hurt whoever hurt me. I think that's a human instinct, otherwise we wouldn't have "an eye for an eye" as one of the oldest lessons of civilized society.

I've long sought to indulge my deep-seated villainy, to let my rage run unfettered, but, unfortunately, years of feeling victimized have made it impossible for me to truly be a villain. Having suffered at numerous points in my life, I've developed an enormous, incredibly annoying capacity for empathy. Hurting someone because they hurt me always feels like the right thing, the thing I want to do, but I invariably start thinking about why that person hurt me in the first place.

That boy who blocked me, he treated me like an asshole for months, but I kept giving him the benefit of the doubt because I didn't and couldn't know what he was going through. Even when he blocked me, I understood why, though it enraged me.

It's the understanding that gets me. Rage sets in and I'm firing on all vengeful cylinders, but once I place myself in my proposed victim's footsteps, my will to destroy dissipates. I'd be a terrible villain, I'm sad to say.

But I have found a way to monetize my victimhood. And you're reading it. People have been reading and sharing and commenting on my victimhood for years. Because it never seemed fair to me that I should suffer and not get anything out of it. By turning my pain into art and into profit, without deliberately hurting anyone—save for a few white boys who blocked me, but that's the stuff of petty crooks, not supervillains—I've been able to relinquish my own feelings of victimhood.

Despite wanting to be a villain, I'm the hero of my own story.

8

GIFTED

THE HOURS BY Michael Cunningham is one of my favorite works of art. From the book to the film to the opera, I've consumed it all. I read *Mrs. Dalloway*, which plays a central part in the narrative in *The Hours*, and other works by Virginia Woolf, intrigued and awakened by the vigor of her genius. And that's what appealed to me about *The Hours*: its treatment of the burden of genius. How Virginia Woolf's brilliance eventually killed her—her brilliance or her mental illness. They were one and the same, because all geniuses are mad, no? But *The Hours* was such a romantic picture of her genius and the genius of Richard, the poet dying of AIDS who simply "wanted to write about everything," to be able to describe the immensity of life and joy and sadness, who kills himself rather than lose what's left of his mind. In the quiet of my own mind, in the privacy it affords, I have fancied myself a genius, or at least touched by its madness. I expected myself to someday prove my genius to the world, to live up to the greatness I nurtured internally. The work necessary to provide its full evidence. Because what genius declares themselves a genius, besides Kanye West?

But didn't geniuses make their genius known early in life? I was fascinated by the story of Arthur Rimbaud, the queer French poet *enfant terrible* credited with revolutionizing poetry as a teenager before walking away from it all to travel the world, performing odd jobs, never to write again. That was genius. I wasn't that. I also wasn't, like Virginia Woolf or Arthur Rimbaud, white. White genius was allowed to develop in a way that Black genius never was, and to this day the disparities remain. Affirmative action was supposed to be a remedy to this, but thanks to the rumors of racism's death being greatly exaggerated, much like Demi Moore's Molly, *it's in danger, girl.*

Black genius was cultivated in spite of society, never because of it. There are geniuses on the block and in the projects and in prisons who will simply never get a chance to realize their full potential. What a tragedy. What a missed opportunity. Racism's greatest achievement is retarding the progress of a society.

I hadn't the ideal circumstances, but I made the most of them. Yet, twenty came and went, and I hadn't revolutionized anything. My window for becoming an *enfant terrible* behind me, I still believed I had a gift worth sharing. That I was what I had been labeled as a child: gifted.

The Hours spoke to me because I, too, wanted to describe the immensity of it all. And at times I felt myself losing my grip under the burden of my own expectations. While I had a passing belief in my own genius, I had always received affirmations that would stroke my ego. From being in advanced classes and gifted programs and graduating with honors, to when I started writing and the cavalier way people would use "brilliant" when describing me or my work. "Brilliant" is an overused word like "legendary" or "iconic" and should be reserved for those truly deserving, not some baby queen with one serviceable bop and a couple viral TikToks, or whatever the kids are talking about these days.

Did I think I was deserving of being called brilliant? I sure fucking did. It was incredibly validating, especially during all the times I thought I would never be recognized as a genius, or as brilliant, gifted, or talented. There were times I thought I'd simply continue to toil away in obscurity, just another would-be genius crushed beneath his own hubris, my talent proving no match for my ambition.

AMERICA HAS A way of destroying Black brilliance (Malcolm X, MLK Jr., Fred Hampton, Zora Neale Hurston, Nina Simone, Whitney Houston, etc., etc.), if it acknowledges its existence at all. The very idea of genius is a revolution. A revolution of thought, of culture, of society. To be a Black revolutionary is to be a Black genius, and to be a Black genius is to be a Black revolutionary. America may have been founded on revolution, but it hates the idea within its own borders. No, maintenance of the status quo, the preservation of law and order, the upholding of tradition, are in the best interests of keeping the disenfranchised so. This reinforces the sacred traditions of white supremacy.

I'll never forgive how gleeful they were. "They" being the

tabloids, the media, people who had unashamedly loved her who somehow forgot they had, or chose to forget. I'll never forgive how gleeful they were at Whitney Houston's downfall. Hers was a transcendent talent, a form of genius in itself. A gift, unparalleled. As were her interpretive skills. She was one of the first Black artists MTV played, because she was undeniable. For a time, she was America's princess, perfect, happy, with a megawatt smile and a mind-blowing voice. She was already huge when *The Bodyguard* hit, but that movie skyrocketed her to another level altogether, to a rarefied space in which it's difficult to breathe.

And she suffocated. And how gleeful they were at her very public downfall: "CRACK" in bold letters in headlines on even bolder tabloids, the interviews, the reality show, the rehab stints, the attempted comeback, and finally the sad death in a hotel bathtub. Her voice still sends shivers down my spine, still makes me believe, just maybe, that there's a god. And then I think about that sadistic glee. America's Black princess, too talented, too successful, too uppity, brought low. And kicked while she was down. Sure, everyone loves her now, the years of laughing at her addiction and her struggles forgotten in favor of the good times, the music, the shivers down all those spines. But I'll never forget. And I'll never forgive.

Nina Simone refused to be destroyed. She was a destroyer. The epitome of the Black genius as Black revolutionary. "An artist's duty, as far as I'm concerned, is to reflect the times," Simone said. "As far as I'm concerned, it's their choice, but I *choose* to reflect the times and situations in which I find myself." She not only sang about civil rights; she also became deeply involved in the movement. But, like so many Black artists who love this country despite the glaring lack of reciprocity, she grew heartbroken at the stagnant pace of progress and left the US.

She rebelled constantly, against America, against her fans, against herself. But she would not bow, she would not be broken. She left America as an act of self-preservation, as her friend James Baldwin did, as Josephine Baker had before them. It's not just that Europe and other parts of the world were less racist than America—they were less racist, kind of, but theirs was also a different kind of racism. In Europe, racism isn't as much of a governing principle and a baked-in ideology as it is here in the States. These artists moved to Europe because their genius was appreciated abroad. Paris may have fallen in love with Baker, but the St. Louis native was a foreigner in her home country and would've probably remained in obscurity if she had remained here.

Little Richard exploded like, as he loved to refer to himself, a quasar in 1956. He revolutionized a dangerously kinetic style of music that came to be known as rock and roll. Black, queer, flamboyant, sexy, and, above all, talented, Little Richard was a revolution on his own. His music literally broke down racial barriers, as teenagers, both Black and white, tore down the dividing ropes at his concerts, mingling with one another, and thus greatly upsetting the status quo. There was no such thing as a rock star before Little Richard. And every rock star who followed was an imitation.

Still, the artist spent most of his life fighting for the recognition of what he had accomplished. While he changed music with songs like "Tutti Frutti," white artists Pat Boone and Elvis Presley sold far more copies of that song than he did. And the latter would come to be known as the King of Rock and Roll, an honorific that erased Little Richard's foundational contributions to the art form. Adding insult to injury, at the height of his success, Little Richard broke his contract to pursue life as a minister, thus losing royalties, present and future, for all the songs he had written and performed.

Black artists and intellectuals aren't afforded the generosity of the label "genius" as much as their white counterparts. Our accomplishments are often accredited to some white benefactor in the background, or some quirk of fate, or unholy combination of god-given talent, discipline, and hard work. That just makes it easier to steal our gifts without proper compensation, to water them down, to whiten them up, to make them more palatable for more mainstream (read: white) audiences. No one would've called Whitney a genius when she was alive. She didn't write her own songs. She was the progeny of a heritage of great singers including her mother, Cissy Houston, and cousins Dionne Warwick and Leontyne Price. And she was the protégée of Clive Davis.

But her genius is undeniable. And her talent changed American culture. It changed the way people sing. Of course, it would do the world good if folks realized that not everyone has the range for an abundance of melisma. Sometimes it's okay to just get the damn song out. But Whitney was America, for a brief, shining moment. America, as a concept and a country, peaked with her performance of "The Star-Spangled Banner" at the 1991 Super Bowl. A Black woman sang the definitive version of the nation's anthem, making it her goddamn own. A so-so song made better by the omission of multiple verses, including some with direct references to slavery, made incredible by a queer Black woman, the manifestation of the American Dream or Nightmare, depending on whom you ask. Her interpretation of that song is nothing short of genius. Because no one else has done it better, and most anyone who attempts it sings it like Whitney. Well, tries to. God bless 'em.

But because Whitney's talent was so tremendous, the rigor behind it was diminished. Genius usually isn't associated with rigor. As if ideas fall freshly out of the air. I interviewed Viola Davis while she was promoting *The Woman King*. She's one of the most intense and electrifying actors to ever occupy the screen. But she was adamant that those performances always cost you something. I remember when I first saw her in 2008's *Doubt*. She's in the movie for like ten minutes, tops. But that's all she needed to launch herself into the pantheon of the greatest living actors. Opposite Meryl Fucking Streep, no less. Davis just acts with her whole body, with her whole being; it's in the way she walks, the way those magnificent eyes plead for truth, no matter how brutal it may be. Davis has accomplished more than any other Black actress in Hollywood history, deservedly, but I always think of that other greatest living Black actress, Angela Bassett.

So much was made of her arms in *What's Love Got to Do with It*, the Tina Turner biopic in which she turns in truly one of film's most amazing performances. And the rigor that went into that performance, the research she did, the way she closely studied Turner's movements, the way she spoke, how it was so much more than mere imitation, but embodiment. But one of my favorite performances of Bassett's is in Spike Lee's criminally underrated 2015 film *Chi-Raq*, in which she plays Miss Helen Worthy, a pillar of her community in Chicago's South Side.

It's one scene. She's in her garden when an insurance salesman comes up to her. She's patient, respectful, even kind at first, until she realizes this insurance salesman is selling insurance for inner-city boys who may be the victims of violence. Angela Bassett listens so beautifully. The way her eyes shift and her demeanor changes when this man shows his proverbial ass and her eruption into rage, righteous and riotous . . . it's fucking thrilling.

Bassett reportedly stays in character while on set, a method often accredited to "genius" white actors like Robert DeNiro, Marlon Brando, and Meryl Streep. Bassett, who has a master's from Yale, is never lumped in with those geniuses; her filmography is not as monumental, though her performances are.

All everyone wants to know is how she got those arms! The same way Michelle Obama got her much-buzzed-about arms: carrying the burdens of a brilliant Black woman in America.

BECAUSE I CAME from a foreign country, I was put into remedial classes when I entered the American school system via Poughkeepsie's Clinton Elementary. So named after Governor George Clinton and sadly not Parliament Funkadelic's George Clinton, as I would learn in time, to my great disappointment. I hated being in those classes and didn't understand why I was in them, since my precociousness was already a thorn in the side of my entire family. But it was regular protocol, and I eventually "graduated" to whatever grade I was supposed to be in.

I don't remember if it was kindergarten, but I do remember fearing for my life at the prospect of failing kindergarten because I couldn't tie my shoes. My motor skills have always been shit. I remember being so frustrated that I couldn't figure it out, I started crying. I was so fucking smart at everything else, as my kindergarten teacher told my mother, but since I was a kid who found his extraordinariness in feeling smart and being told how smart I was, feeling dumb made me lose all confidence in myself.

It still does. I hate not being able to understand something. I hate feeling dumb. It feels as if I've been found out, exposed for being not as smart as I think, or as I hope everyone else thinks I am. I placed all my value in being the smartest. I wasn't athletic, I wasn't popular. I was cute, but all . . . well, most kids are cute. But everyone at that age is looking for ways to stand out, their world having gone from their family to a classroom to a whole school. As their world expands, their place in the center of it is ever diminished. Some people are fine to recede into the background, while some people crave being the center, for all eyes to be on them. And we call those people stars. Or megalomaniacs. Same thing. If I wasn't the smartest, then I was just like everybody else. No one put pressure on me to get good grades because no one had to. I put all the pressure on myself. My aunt would, from time to time, give me the "Make sure you're doing well in school" talk, but my general attitude toward that was, *Bitch, do you know who you're talking to?*

Once my mother realized she didn't have to worry about me in school—I actually *liked* going to school (NERD!)—my achievements lost their luster. *Oh, another 100 on a test, good for you.* Anything less than perfect and I was known to cry, my fragile scholastic ego shattered. Unsurprisingly, kids made fun of me because I would cry at a 92 when they were staring blankly at a 65. I can't say I blamed them. I was an unapologetic teacher's pet. I craved the validation of that tall person at the front of the room more than I craved validation from my mother or anyone else. And if they were immune to my obsequious charms, I could at least win them over with my academic record.

At the end of every school year at Clinton Elementary, we took aptitude tests, which measured our skills in reading, math, and whatever the hell they taught us, against all the other kids our age in the country. I looked forward to those tests because I would regularly rank in the highest percentile. My teacher might call me over and show me my test and point out how I had scored in the 98th or 99th percentile in something that probably wasn't math. I was fine at math, but words were my strong suit. Even as I got older and I wasn't the smartest kid in my class anymore, I was always the strongest writer.

There was this profile on ABC about Ronan Farrow going to college at ten years old or something crazy like that. I was so jealous. I wanted to go to college at ten. I wanted to be a prodigy; I wanted to be profiled by Diane Sawyer. At the end of fifth grade, my teacher, Ms. Howard, asked my mom if she could take me on a trip to Boston as a reward for being her top student. She was a young Black woman with large glasses and an enviable sense of style—it was all culottes and chunky turtle-necks with her, in autumnal shades, gorgeous. With some not-so-gentle prodding from me, my mother agreed. Since coming to America, I had only been to about two places: New York City, where we flew into, and Poughkeepsie, some sixty miles north of the city in the Hudson Valley. Boston was in a whole other state!

I was so excited, but also nervous, because even at ten, I worried about the awkward silence of a long car ride. Sure, I had seen Ms. Howard nearly every day for the past nine months, but that was never a one-on-one situation. *What will we talk about?!* I wondered. But teachers know how to talk to kids, that's literally their job, and before long my anxiety was put at ease for the five hours or so we drove to Boston. Ms. Howard wanted to expand my horizons. The world can feel small, suffocating, hopeless living in Poughkeepsie. And here was Boston. It wasn't as big and busy and intimidating as New York, but it had all that centuries-old architecture, all that history haunting the air, all the blood that had soaked the streets. For a city baptized in blood, it sure was pretty.

At Boston Common, Ms. Howard and I took in the memorial to Crispus Attucks and the Boston Massacre, a statue of a woman holding aloft broken chains and crushing the British crown beneath her granite heel. This being an educational trip, Ms. Howard took the opportunity to quiz me on who Crispus Attucks was. A formerly enslaved man, Attucks was the first casualty of the Boston Massacre; thus from his blood sprang forth the American Revolution. Attucks was one of the few Black heroes (though his ethnic origins are disputed) not limited for study during Black History Month since his story is directly intertwined with the fight for American independence. Black people, legally not even people at the time, rarely figured in that telling, save for maybe a passing mention of Sally Hemings as proof of the fallibility of the Founding Fathers. But Attucks was the first person to lose his life for a country that had previously kept him shackled, beginning a long tradition of Black sacrifice for a nation resolute in its whiteness.

For a young Black boy, Crispus Attucks was a hero, but for a young Black man he became more of a cautionary tale. As I grew older, my heroes didn't die for this country. They died in defiance of this country. Malcolm X was one of those Black geniuses on the block, in the projects, in prison, who, through the force of his own intelligence, became one of the preeminent thinkers of twentieth-century America. Short shrift is given to the genius of just being able to survive, let alone *thrive*, in America as a Black person. Or the genius of defying expectations and overcoming extraordinary circumstances. But with the burden of just surviving, let alone thriving, it's often impossible to cultivate genius in any other realm, not when all of one's energy goes to getting through the fucking day.

THAT TRIP TO Boston meant so much to me. I knew I was special, but I rarely got to feel special, living in that one-bedroom apartment on Main Street, the small black-and-white television in the room I shared with my mother my only outlet to the world at large. Ms. Howard emailed me out of the blue one day a few years back. She had thought of me and just

Googled my name. "I am Miss Howard and I taught a Lester Brathwaite in fifth grade at Gov. Clinton Elementary School, room 16. I took him on a trip to Boston once and I just wanted to know if it is you," she wrote. It's so rare you get to thank, as an adult, the people who made a profound impact on you as a child. I was overjoyed to have that opportunity.

And I'm sure teachers rarely get the chance to see the fruits of their labor in the adults whom they inspired as children. I thanked Ms. Howard for taking me on that trip and for the impact she had on my life. I bragged that I was a writer living in Brooklyn, that I was "more or less living my dream." I figured she'd like to hear that, and it was true, more or less. "I am so proud of you. I never forgot you," she wrote me back. "I always knew that you would be successful. You were always a very gifted writer, so I am not at all surprised to see that you write professionally."

She was "so proud" of me . . . it was almost like hearing that from my mother. I never got to hear my mother say that to me as an adult. I had never thought I needed to hear that from her, or to know that she was proud of me, because I was a bad bitch, I had done this and that and the other by myself. What approval did I need? I might not have needed it, but I cherished hearing that from Ms. Howard. Teachers are fucking awesome.

WITH TEACHERS LIKE Ms. Howard who believed in me, encouraged me, recommended me for gifted programs or for special awards, I really thought I was special and could and would do great things. As I got further along in school, I continued to feel special, though perhaps for the wrong reasons. By the time I was taking Advanced Placement classes in high school, I was one of two, maybe more, maybe not, Black students in a scholastic sea of white. I was special because I was a minority who excelled academically.

I felt the pressure to prove I was smart not just for myself but for all the other Black kids who didn't make it that far in high school, because there were a lot more of us back in the honors middle school classes. Slowly, year by year, they fell away, and there was sometimes just me. I feared giving the wrong answer, even when I knew I was right. The doubt threatened to overcome me. Why, I wondered, were there so many white kids in these classes? Were they just smarter than Black kids? Or were they just better at taking tests? Did they have some advantage that we didn't, most likely money? These thoughts nagged me every day in my AP classes. But I was determined to best them any way I could. I was determined to be a sterling example of my race. The Sidney Poitier of Poughkeepsie High School.

Poitier, the first Black man to win a Best Actor Oscar, was saddled with the burden of representing all of Black America during the '60s. He was then the community's only leading actor of his stature in Hollywood. He garnered both praise and criticism for the roles he played, often portraying the exalted, gooder-than-good Negro. That is, until in one of cinema's most satisfying scenes he slapped a white man as take-no-guff detective Virgil Tibbs. That role in 1967's Best Picture winner, *In the Heat of the Night*, was an outlier for Poitier. That same year he had also starred in the popular *To Sir, with Love*, as a respectable Black teacher to a class of predominantly white delinquent kids, and in *Guess Who's Coming to Dinner* as a respectable Black doctor with the gall to marry his way into Spencer Tracy and Katharine Hepburn's very white family.

Virgil Tibbs slapping a white man who tried to put him in his place as an uppity nigger was wish fulfillment for Black people all over America that year. Until that point, Poitier had been the unimpeachable Negro, for the sake of white people. He wasn't an example for Black people to follow so much as for white people, a sterling example of his race. Being a Black person in predominantly white spaces often leaves me feeling like Sidney Poitier, both in wanting to be of unimpeachable character and in wanting to slap the shit out of a white man.

For whom, however, was I being this sterling example? For these rich white kids? My teacher? Myself? I really thought those rich white kids would think less of me—and by extension less of all the other Black kids in school—if I was anything short of exemplary. And maybe they did, implicitly or not. Or maybe they didn't have to think about things like that at all. Perhaps not being told or otherwise made aware of having to be "twice as good to get half as far" gave them the freedom to think about other things, the confidence to be wrong, and the knowledge that their opinion was valid.

I think it's easier to be a genius when you're young because the world doesn't expect too much from you, so when you exceed those minimal expectations, grandly, then the superlatives start flying. To be a genius in your more advanced years, you have to continue to revolutionize, when revolution is primarily the domain of the young. That's why some prodigies flicker out so early. Maybe Arthur Rimbaud had just said and done all he had to say and do. Genius is not infinite.

In order to prove my worth, to myself most of all, I thought I had to come out with something revolutionary by a certain age. Twenty-three seemed to be the cutoff, maybe twenty-five. Any older and both I and my accomplishment would be less impressive. Lauryn Hill came out with *The Miseducation of Lauryn Hill* at twenty-three. By twenty-three, Stevie Wonder had already produced several certified masterpieces. And unlike Lauryn Hill, Wonder wrote, produced, and performed nearly all the instrumentation. In popular culture, there's probably no more pure embodiment of a "genius" than Stevie Wonder. And nigga was blind the entire time. *Songs in the Key of Life* (released when he was twenty-six) is, for my money, the one album that could and should represent the height of human achievement for future generations, for the aliens, whatever.

Hill was credited as the sole writer and producer on her *Miseducation*, a move that prompted a lawsuit against her, her management, and the record label. Her team claimed that the credit was the decision of the label in an attempt to market her as a Wonder or a Prince. A true genius. A prodigy. The rest of the writers and producers, however, didn't take kindly to that and sued, and won, to get their proper credit. Does that take away from the brilliance of *The Miseducation of Lauryn Hill*? A little bit.

I was incredibly impressed when I thought that Hill had written and produced this entire album by the time she was twenty-three. While the fact that she didn't do it alone doesn't take away from the brilliance of the music (that's timeless), it does take away from the legacy of Hill's virtuosity. The same questions that dogged Lauryn Hill now dog Beyoncé; that is, how much of her work is her, and how much is it the work of everyone else? Beyoncé is the most important, ambitious, and consistent artist of my generation. While I try to abstain from stan culture and don't consider myself part of the at-times cult-like Hive, I'm a big fan. But even I question how much of her work is hers alone.

These are questions I don't really bother with when it comes to white artists. Or, for that matter, male artists. Beyoncé's music has been transformative for me, and as I see it, her artistic vision can be divided into three eras. There's the millennial pop diva with something to prove, from her solo debut, *Dangerously in Love* in 2003, to 2008's *I Am . . . Sasha Fierce*. Already known as a writer and producer, she co-wrote and co-produced the majority of *Dangerously*. She was twenty-two. That's impressive. But like every album she produces, it's seen as a production, incorporating multiple songwriters and producers. As she's gotten more successful, and as her music has gotten greater, the number of contributors has also increased. While she's still credited as co-writer and co-producer on nearly every if not all tracks, there's a veritable army behind her.

As a result, despite four nominations, Beyoncé has never won an Album of the Year Grammy. Despite releasing *the* album of the year multiple times. In comparison, Taylor Swift, noted as a singer-songwriter, has won three Album of the Year Grammys, her first at just twenty. She was the youngest artist to win Album of the Year until Billie Eilish won at just eighteen.

Eilish wrote the majority of the album and her brother, Finneas O'Connell, produced it. The Recording Academy respects "artistry." And often their "true" artists are white.

A Black woman hasn't won Album of the Year since Hill. Had the fact that she hadn't solely written and produced the album come out before voting commenced, she probably wouldn't have won the top prize, despite *Miseducation* being *the* album of the year. The controversy around it alone would make it anathema to the Recording Academy, but then, her feat wouldn't be as commendable, as award-worthy. Beyoncé will never win an Album of the Year award unless she writes and produces the album by her own damn self. And while I'm sure she could, she doesn't want to and I don't want her to. Have you heard "Cuff It"? It has three hundred (okay, nine) writers and is worth every last one of them.

But even when a Black artist does write and produce and occupy that white singer-songwriter space, because it is a white space, they aren't guaranteed respect. Mariah Carey's been talking about being a songwriter first and a singer second since the beginning of her career. But because she's a woman, and because she's a Black woman, for years she wasn't given respect as a songwriter despite penning or co-penning eighteen of her nineteen number one hits. Speaking of Grammy losses, at the 1996 Grammys, Carey was expected to clean up with six nominations, including Album of the Year for *Daydream*. One word: "Fantasy." She lost all six awards, with the top honor going to singer-songwriter Alanis Morissette's *Jagged Little Pill*.

Of course, awards are bullshit, but Black artists have always strived for respect from institutions that they don't really need. Is Angela Bassett any less of an actress because she doesn't have a competitive Oscar? (An honorary is cute, but . . . c'mon.) They'll give those things out to just about anybody these days. Jared Leto? C'mon! But those institutions say that they're important, despite the public's growing apathy toward them. Interest in, and ratings for, the Academy Awards has been on a steep decline for more than a decade. And the Grammys are irrelevant. They just like inviting all the top Black talent to make their show interesting and maybe give them a few small awards to keep them "happy" while doling out the big awards to white acts. It's blatant disrespect, and some artists refuse to play along. Drake, the Weeknd, and Kanye West, among others, have been boycotting the Grammys. If only Beyoncé refused to show up to another ceremony, as she certainly should, the Grammys would lose whatever's left of their credibility. But then she would be criticized as a sore loser, despite losing graciously again, and again, and again.

After *Miseducation*, Lauryn Hill dropped out. She was expected to be this savior of music; she was heralded as *the* talent to watch in the coming millennium, a self-proclaimed "rapper slash actress, more powerful than two Cleopatras." But years went by and . . . nothing. Then she resurfaced with a double album and accompanying TV special, *MTV Unplugged No. 2.0*. Both the show and the album were divisive. Its unnerving intimacy, with Hill breaking into candid soliloquy and occasionally breaking down in tears, was uncomfortable for people to watch. Which was the whole point. Hill had reinvented herself as, would you believe it, a singer-songwriter, sporting a guitar she was still teaching herself how to play. Her music was raw, incredibly personal, but it was hers. All hers.

It was as if she wanted to prove that she had the chops and that she didn't need the trappings of the industry. It was not a commercial release. There were no hits to come off it, at least not until Kanye West sampled "Mystery of Iniquity" for his "All Falls Down." Hill could've followed up with another big studio album, which is what everyone wanted her to do, but instead she did what she wanted to do, what she had to do. Hill has garnered comparisons to Nina Simone, and it started with *Unplugged*. It's that kind of fierce genius that refuses to be defined or confined, reflecting the times in an unexpected, even volatile way.

Since *Unplugged*, Hill hasn't released any new material of consequence. She had grown disillusioned with the recording industry, as nearly every artist inevitably does and has, and walked away from it all. She was hardly the first Black genius to shun the spotlight for the sake of self-preservation. Sometimes you just have to choose yourself over the wants and desires of everyone else. Something Nina Simone certainly understood. So, rather appropriately, Hill reemerged in 2015 on the soundtrack for the Nina Simone documentary, *What Happened, Miss Simone?*, singing six songs, including a cover of Simone's "Feeling Good." Simone had laid the template from which Hill had built her own path to freedom. At least her version of freedom.

TO BE YOUNG, gifted, and Black is a lovely, precious dream, but it's also a burden, even a curse. To be young, gifted, and

Black is to see the world in possibilities. But the older you get, the less possible things may seem, and looking back, you wonder how you were able to do any of what you did in the first place. Or maybe you regret not doing more, having realized that sometimes the only obstacle in your way . . . was yourself.

I wanted to create and perform and be loved for my work. But as I got older, while I was impressed with what I was able to accomplish, when saddled with the complexities of reality, I was disappointed to fall short of my own expectations. I was also wary of the passage of time, the hours disappearing before my very eyes. How many self-styled great Black artists struggled in futility to fulfill their potential, only to succumb to madness, or poverty, or self-destruction from a combination of the two? How many of those minds were truly great, but chained by their circumstances? What tragedies. What missed opportunities.

It takes so much to realize one's own potential, so much drive and determination, and the further one is from the mainstream, the more infallible one must be on the path to that realization. Of course, luck has something to do with it. I felt I was lucky to just have survived and made it out of Poughkeepsie, to make it to thirty when for years I romanticized an early death, a brilliant flame snuffed out too early. Artists who die young get off easy. They're always remembered as greater than they were due to all the things they were never able to do. Perish the thought they had given all they had to give.

A part of me put so much stock in accomplishing something "great" in my youth because I feared I was already living on borrowed time. Touched by death so early and unexpectedly, I anticipated death at every turn, and then there was the cavalier way I went about my life, snorting whatever anyone put in my face, no questions asked. The drugs and debauchery, however, were also part of the frustration and the romanticism of an "artist's life." I thought it my right to destroy myself as part of the creative process. I found validation in people like Rimbaud, who was reportedly a fucking little monster during his most productive years, seducing the older, married writer Paul Verlaine, drinking absinthe, smoking opium and hash all over Europe. Verlaine eventually shot his young, impetuous lover in a drunken rage, putting an end to their affair as a bullet to the arm often does.

Naturally, I romanticized that kind of gorgeous, lived chaos, particularly because it was so fucking gay, proving that faggots have always faggoted and will continue to faggot, in perpetuity. Moreover, Rimbaud's youthful rebelliousness worked, to my naïve eyes. It added to his appeal, perhaps not in his own time, but for future faggots and would-be rebel geniuses. But Rimbaud gave it up to live a steady, normal life, perhaps disillusioned with poetry, with his own genius, with his suffering. Did he ever find happiness?

I was content to be the ultimate sacrifice to my art. I was *supposed* to be miserable. I was *supposed* to succumb to my demons. That was what artists did, wasn't it? Virginia Woolf walking into a river with stones in her pocket. Hendrix and Joplin and Morrison and Cobain and Winehouse all dead, famously, at twenty-seven.

The role of the artist seemed to be to change the world, then get crushed by it. Or maybe it was that one couldn't change the world without paying some consequence for doing so. I foolishly but fervently related suffering to genius and profound creativity. The success I sought was thus a validation of my suffering. Proof positive I hadn't gone through this, that, and the other for no reason at all. That being Black, and queer, and poor wasn't a hindrance to my success but the reason for it.

My idea of success, however, changed. Out of necessity. Surviving was a success in and of itself. Or as Dorian Corey, the world-weary drag queen and one-woman Greek chorus of the 1990 documentary *Paris Is Burning*, says with marksman-like precision in the film's epilogue:

> *I always had hopes of being a big star. But as you get older, you aim a little lower. Everybody wants to make an impression, some mark upon the world. Then you think, you've made a mark on the world if you just get through it, and a few people remember your name. Then you've left a mark. You don't have to bend the whole world. I think it's better to just enjoy it. Pay your dues, and just enjoy it. If you shoot an arrow and it goes real high, hooray for you.*

I never wanted to aim lower. In truth, I still feel like I can do whatever I want, become whatever I dream, because I have to believe it. I have to have unwavering, almost superhuman, confidence in my own bad bitchery in order to keep going. I need that confidence to continue on this foolhardy quest of being an artist, of being a writer, of living for ideas. But believing is not the same as doing. I know in theory I can do anything, but I know in reality I am only capable of doing so much. When I started to accept reality was when I started feeling defeated by life. Reality was, after all, "something you rise above," in the words of the always down-to-earth Liza Minnelli.

That rising above was also the ethos of *Paris Is Burning*. That one need not accept the reality one is given. The subjects of this landmark documentary, drag queens and gender-nonconforming people of color living in '80s New York City, faced myriad obstacles to simply existing: poverty, racism, homophobia, transphobia, AIDS, governmental indifference. This is what I mean when I write about the genius of Black survival. They turned their method of survival—which is exactly what ballroom has always been—into a culture-shifting art form.

Black kweens have been throwing balls in Harlem going back to the late 1860s. They started off as charity masquerade galas with men in female drag and women in male drag, and prizes were given out for the most handsome drag king and the "most perfect feminine body displayed by an impersonator." Imagine being able to embrace any sort of queer identity just a scant few years after you had been constitutionally recognized as a human being.

There is a need for fantasy in Black queer life, whether as a means of survival or an expression of our defiantly boundless joy. Fantasy is an escape, it is an aspiration, it can even lead to self-actualization. Fake it till ya make it. The performance of this fantasy—which is often a fantasy of white life and its attendant freedoms, luxuries, etc.—is done so elegantly, so eleganza-ly, as to always attract white audiences. By the 1920s, the "fairies" or "faggots" balls, as they were called, had white folks, already drawn by the siren call of jazz, dancing with Black folks and gawking at the drag queens.

There was an initial wave of mainstream (that is, as always: white) interest in ballroom—from Jennie Livingston shooting the bulk of her doc in 1986; to the 1989 release of Malcolm McLaren's "Deep in Vogue," crescendoing with Madonna's "Vogue" in March of 1990; the eventual wide theatrical release of *Paris Is Burning* the following year; and the interest it piqued in its immediate aftermath. During that time, the members of the ballroom community did their best to cash in on the new-found attention. But the stigma of AIDS and the rampant conservatism of the post-Reagan years, coupled with the fickle nature of the mainstream's interest, didn't bring them the fame around which they had built their fantasies.

It's funny, though. Dorian Corey died in 1993. A number of the subjects of the documentary died either violently or from AIDS-related causes, yet their influence has long outlived them. Their words are mantras, slogans, and some faggots' entire personalities. RuPaul—despite being more of a downtown kween, in style and location, when most of the balls were uptown—has built a media empire on ballroom and drag. RuPaul has always been clever. He changed his downtown, drag-punk style into a more glamazon, high-fashion version of drag. This brand-new Ru was more in line with the rich white woman fantasy that had been born in the ballroom, and his 1993 single, "Supermodel (You Better Work)" made him a post-*Paris* drag superstar. Ru was the more polished, more palatable version of Pepper LaBeija, one of the main figures in *Paris Is Burning*.

Not coming from the balls, RuPaul's appeal was able to

outlast interest generated by the documentary. But his career waned nonetheless until the first season of a cheaply produced but highly entertaining drag queen competition show in 2008. From the Vaseline-lensed, duct-taped gowns of that first season, *RuPaul's Drag Race* became a global phenomenon.

Incorporating elements of ballroom (such as reading, balls, and runway categories) within the competition, *Drag Race* created its own bastardized version of ballroom. If you say "death-drop" around a ballroom kween, they will slice you from tip to taint with their side-eyes. It's called a "dip." And "boots the house down" was never in coinage before, like, 2018. But while bastardized, *RuPaul's Drag Race* keeps ballroom culture alive by introducing it to newer generations and audiences, all while opening the door for other media that is more authentic to its original spirit, such as the ballroom competition show *Legendary* and the groundbreaking FX drama *Pose*.

Dorian Corey, Pepper LaBeija, and so many of the brilliant talent featured in *Paris Is Burning* didn't live long enough to see that their arrows didn't stop soaring; those arrows continued flying higher than they could ever have expected. I guess reality can be something you rise above; you just might not live long enough to see it. The gift and curse of genius is that it's always ahead of its time and therefore risks going unrecognized.

EVERY FEW MONTHS I like to take a mushroom trip, to realign myself and the way I'm seeing the world. The last time was quite the doozy. I had a crisis of conscience about writing. I had finally gotten around to reading Zora Neale Hurston's

Their Eyes Were Watching God and was floored by its beauty. My interest in Hurston piqued, I did a little research on the old girl. Famously written in seven weeks (or so), and with such vivid language, brilliantly rendered characters, and a compelling story, surely *Their Eyes Were Watching God* was a work of genius. And the forcefulness of its genius must have been apparent at the time of its publication in 1937. Surely.

It wasn't. Hurston, I was depressed to find out, died broke and forgotten at age sixty-nine in 1960. What was the point, I wondered, of creating something so wonderful only to be forgotten in your lifetime? But the book lived on. Her work lives on. With this weighing heavily on my mind, I took my shrooms and cried naked on the floor listening to Stevie Wonder's *Songs in the Key of Life*, filled with the joy of his genius. I sat on the beach in Provincetown, home of Michael Cunningham, and wept at the beauty of a sunset, when my favorite quote from Cunningham's *The Hours* came to me. It was about thinking a moment is the beginning of happiness when in fact, in cruel reality, it *is* happiness. This, I thought, looking at the beautiful burning red sun at the end of the world, was happiness. This was what I'd been working my way toward. This brief moment that I would carry with me long after I'd left that place. And so I cried. I've cried only a handful of times in my adult life.

And then I realized why I write. It was for these moments, when I feel at peace with the universe, when I feel a part of the world without the need to bend it or to bend to it. These moments of indescribable beauty compel me to *describe* them, to capture them, to make the ephemeral somehow permanent. If this is happiness, I need to preserve it, disseminate it, honor it the best way I know how. It's a gift to be able to do so. Sometimes I stop to think the little gay boy inside of me would gag at what I've been able to accomplish and who I've become. It may not be exactly what we imagined, but to come this far, to live life on our own terms, to be able to be happy, to have moments shaking with joy, to write and write well for a living—it's what I've always wanted. I mean, an Oscar would be nice, but I never have to give up on my fantasies. After all, reality hasn't beat me quite yet.

I've come to terms with the fact that I probably won't change the world, Beyoncé having taken the career I really wanted. But she's doing fine with it, I guess, it's in good hands, I'm not bitter, whatever. I may not change the world, but I can experience as much of it as possible, divorced from any one institution's or person's idea of success or genius. Including my own. It's more than enough to just enjoy being alive.

9

SILENCE

If you're silent about your pain, they'll kill you and say you enjoyed it.

 —Zora Neale Hurston, *Their Eyes Were Watching God*

MY AUNT'S VOICE, faint and scratchy, crackled over the phone. My brother had woken me up, or maybe I was already awake, to tell me she wanted to talk to me. I immediately knew why she was calling. I had been preparing for it. I hate to be caught off guard, so I try to prepare for everything, to the best of my ability. My aunt sounded tired. She had been dealing with the hospitals, both Vassar Brothers in Poughkeepsie and then Mount Sinai in the city, where, overnight, they had flown my mother days ago, maybe it was weeks. I mess up on the timeline of it all. "It happened so suddenly." Isn't that what they always say?

I knew this phone call would come. My mother's illness was sudden. Pneumonia. People didn't die from pneumonia. Not in the United States. Not in 1999. On the cusp of the millennium. If she had still been in Guyana, then it might have made more sense. But this was the greatest country in the world. They could save her. My brother had taken me aside when we were at Mount Sinai, after we had seen her, so distant and remote in her hospital bed. She had a fifty-fifty shot at survival, the doctors had told him. No one really talked to me. I was not yet fourteen, so they just talked around me, as they had always done. And as I had always done, I pieced the puzzle together myself.

"She could die," Wayne had told me then, and I looked up at him. Silence. I didn't know how he expected me to react. I didn't know how I expected me to react. The school year had just started two months ago, my freshman year of high school. I was excited to become a real, red-blooded, American teenager. I'd make friends and go to parties and learn to drive and, who knows, maybe my mom would get me a used car once I had my license. She didn't drive, so it would behoove both of us to have a car in the family. And the wonders it would do for my social life.

She had talked about finally getting me a computer, through one of those rent-to-own situations from Aaron's, the store we lived above on Main Street. She had bought our beds, hers a queen, mine a twin, and the dining room table that way, and I needed a computer to keep up with the demand of my high school course load. And I would need a car to get to and from school and take her to the supermarket or the mall. So went my reasoning when I would campaign for a car. And of course, I would get a job to help pay for both. I had it all planned out. High school would be my time to blossom. Finally.

Middle school had been rough—it sucked, really. But in high school, I'd shine. My voice had changed, finally, and while I missed hitting those soprano notes, I anticipated what other changes my body would go through. Yes, things would be okay. I would be okay.

My aunt's voice was almost like a stranger's to me. A fifty-fifty chance, they had said. My mother's age was a complicating factor. She was young, the doctors had said, though she had never been young to me. She had me when she was almost forty-two. She was now almost fifty-six. She wasn't too old, the doctor meant, to fight for her life. She could still make it.

My aunt called me that morning, November 2, to tell me my mother hadn't made it. I heard the words and felt them as they washed over me. I stood there holding the phone. Silence. My aunt asked if I had heard her. My mother was dead. I had heard her. I didn't know what to say except, "Okay." Was I supposed to cry? Why couldn't I cry? Did I care at all? What was I supposed to feel? Could I feel, or was I just as numb as my mother's body lying in the morgue at Mount Sinai? The only thing I knew was that I wanted to go to school, to pretend that my life was normal for one more day because it would never be again.

IT'S INHUMAN TO suffer in silence. I used to think it was brave, admirable, even. After all, when Sydney Carton goes to the guillotine in *A Tale of Two Cities*, he's not kicking and screaming, because it's a far, far better thing he does, blah blah

blah. And Jesus faced his suffering like a godlike man. Why shouldn't I? Why shouldn't we all?

So many of us are taught to never complain. It's un-American to show weakness. It's also un-Guyanese, which is where I'm from. Both America and Guyana are former colonies of Great Britain, home of the famed stiff upper lip. They both inherited their stoic suffering from the United Kingdom, a source of countless other atrocities. At the same time, Americans are far less cool and collected, and far less likely to keep calm and carry on. There's a rebelliousness here that will not quite go gently into that good night.

As much as our leaders would like us to remain silent, as silence equals complicity, America is a loud-ass country. You have to speak up in order to be heard, unless you're carrying a big stick, like noted soft-speaker Teddy Roosevelt. Either way, there has to be a force about you that speaks volumes. Immigrants have to learn that the hard way. We come into this country with our own values and beliefs and traditions and are automatically assaulted with the cacophonous American way of life. We have to speak up. And speak American, which is a different language entirely from English.

In this new home, however, we are further silenced as we're forced to assimilate. Thus we retreat into our own little communities, where we're free to speak our language, enjoy our customs, and avoid being persecuted because of our differences. The image of the docile, hardworking immigrant is cliché by now. They're stealing our jobs, the conservatives say. Jobs Americans don't want, the liberals counter, adding, self-righteously, *They keep our country running.* And our country keeps them servile. Those who are here illegally dare not rock the boat, while those who are here legally fear being ostracized and called un-American.

Really, any member of a minority group who questions the evils of America is likely to be accused of being un-American. This accusation comes by way of the only "real" Americans in existence, the whites. And the whites are the loudest voices in the room. I've been in America for the majority of my life, but my voice will never rise to the level of that of a white. But my voice was silenced early on, before I even knew what it meant to be in the loudest country in the world.

WITHIN THAT SILENCE I think I may have felt guilty.

My mother and I were not unique in that we had a complicated, even contentious relationship. She wasn't much for sharing her feelings, and so I wasn't either. She hated when I cried. It seemed everyone hated when I cried. Guyana may be in South America, but culturally, it has more in common with the islands of the West Indies. Parents could be strict, even violent; homosexuality was discouraged; and there was a very narrow definition of what it meant to be a man. Or a boy.

My mother was raising me on her own, and I'm not so sure she had expected to raise a young boy at this late stage in her life. She had already raised my brother and would continue raising him till her death. I wasn't a bad kid by any measure, but precocious kids are annoying. With their questions and their observations and their know-it-all attitudes. There was very little tolerance for children who didn't know their place in most West Indian households. Mine was no exception.

When we were all still living with my aunt and uncle and their three boys, I had once told my mother to shut up. Let me tell you. I hear and see white kids telling their parents to shut up all the time, and I can't help think to myself, *That lucky little shit.* You don't tell adults to shut up among Black people, of any origin. It's not gonna fly. That impudent child might fly across the room. But their insolence will not be tolerated.

So once those words came out of my mouth, it was a mad dash for my life, with my uncle in hot pursuit. "Shut up" was probably just something I heard from my favorite teacher, television, and I had repeated it, as I repeated everything. I was four, so I might not have known how bad it was, and considering who I am and have always been, I might've refused to apologize. Whatever the exact circumstances, I vividly remember running from the dining room, through the kitchen, down the stairs to the basement, my uncle right behind me, until he caught and pinned me against the bookshelf and hit me repeatedly as I wept and wailed. No one, no man, certainly, had ever hit me like that before or since. I remember my uncle hitting me, and I remember no one saying or doing anything about it. Including my mother.

From then on, I knew what was expected of me: silence. Like a good boy, I would be seen and not heard; I wouldn't talk unless spoken to; I would never interrupt an adult; I could never truly express myself. So I turned inward. I hated speaking anyway. I have a stutter that manifests itself now as an inability to speak with the clarity I can only find in the written word. I hate that I tend to mumble and jumble my words together, but it so often feels like something out of my control. It's a weakness that leaves me feeling powerless. I learned, then, that it's easier to remain quiet and appear strong than to speak and reveal weakness. Silence became the refuge my family never could be. Years later I would cut them out of my life completely.

After I had sufficiently learned my lesson, my uncle let my aunt take me to the bathroom to clean up my snot and tears. But I couldn't stop crying. My aunt, exasperated, told me sternly to stop. "Boys don't cry," she informed me, to my great shock. There I was disproving her words, but my aunt was the smartest person I knew, and I loved and respected her so much that she must have been right and I must have been wrong. I tried, for my aunt's sake, to stop the tears, to stop the heaves, coming from deep in my chest, that shook my little body. I used to cry all the time. Tears came so easily. But I was always made to feel that they were wrong, that they didn't belong to me, that boys didn't cry and so I shouldn't cry.

In elementary school, tears were my defense mechanism. If I turned on the waterworks, bullies would leave me alone or someone would go get a teacher and I would be escorted away from danger. But I also cried when I got disappointing test scores. I cried at the slightest provocation. In middle school, I found that my tears invited ridicule. My enormous sensitivity, or as some kids called it, being a fucking pussy, made me even more of a target. So I worked to deaden my emotions.

Eventually, I stopped crying altogether. Through a combination of my conscious decision, the unconscious onset of a numbing depression, and just getting older. Boys are conditioned in adolescence to numb themselves to their own emotions anyway. Not only did I stop crying, I stopped telegraphing my emotions. Because I wasn't raised to talk through my feelings, I internalized them, especially my anger. When I was mad at someone, my default reaction was, and is, to stop talking to them. The good old silent treatment. Not only did I stop talking to whomever had hurt or offended me, but I denied their very existence. I was cold-blooded in my absolute dismissal of people. It just felt easier to cut someone off than it was to talk openly and honestly about how and why they hurt me.

For one, sometimes my anger would overwhelm me to such an extent that I didn't know how to express my emotions, or I was afraid of how they would come out. I'm not one for sugarcoating things, and I never knew how my bluntness would be received. What if I were to say something that would send a fairly innocuous situation down a road of no return? Not that ignoring someone for days or weeks on end led to a better outcome. What often happened was I would be mad for a while and relegate someone to my silence, but once the anger had dissipated or the will to have a conversation had blossomed in my stony heart, I wouldn't know how to end the silence. I usually relied on the other person to break it.

That's the other thing. I was rarely on the receiving end of the silent treatment. Not that my behavior was by any means impeccable, but I endeavored to be beyond reproach. How could I, Lester Fabian Brathwaite, friend, son, and future saint, ever be in the wrong? And even if I was in the wrong, how dare you make me feel that way. For instance, I called my mom a bitch once. In my defense, I didn't think she heard me. A correction: I called my mom a bitch many times, but never within earshot. Except that one time.

We were fighting (about what? Who knows, who cares?) and I had run into the bathroom, where she struck me, which she did from time to time. It was usually nothing more than a slap across the arm or back—you know, somewhere that wouldn't leave a visible bruise. The last thing my mom needed was me running to some well-meaning white teacher and telling them how my mom beat me at home. She only did it as a last resort. This time, however, I overstepped. As she was walking away, I called her the offending epithet, and she heard me.

My mom wasn't the disciplinarian, my uncle was, but the fact that I had the nerve to call her a bitch set off something in her and she hit me repeatedly as I clutched the towel rack. I sobbed. And then I refused to talk to her. I don't know for how long. See, I could pull the silent treatment on everyone else, but when my mother was over it, so was I. Maybe I'd try to extend the period for dramatic effect, but ultimately she'd make me laugh, or take me somewhere, or buy me something I'd been whining about, and all would be forgiven.

Food was the simplest route. Also, I knew I was wrong, and the guilt just ate away at me. After that, my mother never hit me again. I think she felt bad. I also felt bad. I felt bad for calling her a bitch, but really, I felt worse because she had heard me. We had both lost our tempers. She was usually quiet and reserved, but I was acquainted with her other self. She loved to laugh, she loved to dance; there was a fire in her that I inherited.

There was this woman who used to ride the bus at the same time as my mother and me when we went to the supermarket. She was an off-putting woman, terrible wig, but also a terrible attitude. She would bully her way onto the bus and yell at anyone who stood in her way. So she decided to try my mother. Wrong move, ma'am. My mother wouldn't budge. She wasn't afraid of her, and without losing her composure, she told the woman off as I sat quietly next to her, *living*. She shut that woman up and then they kinda became friends. Or at least friendly. Game recognize game, I suppose. I was exceedingly proud of my mother in that moment, for standing up for herself, with all those people on the bus watching. Not like we were on a stage or anything, but sometimes it's easier to just cower rather than stand your ground, especially with an audience present. I get that urge to slink away when faced with any confrontation, but then I remember my mother. If she could stand up for herself, then so could I. It's funny how those little moments in childhood can have such resounding effects. Funny and terrifying. Which is the sweet spot in life.

My mother and I were similar in temperament, which means we got along as often as we didn't. I remember . . . just always being mad at her. I took that old nursery rhyme to heart: "Step on a crack, break your mother's back." There were days I would deliberately step on every crack on the sidewalk in hopes of bringing the promised outcome.

And I would wish her dead. Often. She would make me so mad that I would wish her dead. But mad about what? Did any of it fucking matter? I was probably just being the impudent little shit who had told her to shut up at four years old. My mom and aunt loved to tell the tale of how I screamed and kicked my way into this country, pulling away from my aunt's hand as we walked through the airport, as an example of how rowdy I had been as a child. Yes, we had just been on an impossibly long flight, in coach, and I was definitely tired, cranky, and scared to be ripped from all I knew and shoved into a different country. But they talked of me as if I were a wild colt in need of breaking. And my uncle would be the one to break me. And he did.

His heavy hand imparted on me the fear of god. In time, I would reject both he and Him. I resented my mother. For being poor. For not stopping my uncle from hitting me. For wanting me to be a banker when I wanted so much more. My anger at her most often arose from what she couldn't buy for me. Because she was denying me what I wanted, denying my ability to become whomever I wanted to be. I resented her for saying she would never want a gay child, knowing full well (did she?) that that was exactly what she had.

My uncle had tamed my spirit, but he hadn't broken it. I was still that rowdy, rebellious child, ripping my hand away from authority. I still am . . . and it's exhausting.

I WISHED HER dead so often, and then she was. It wasn't my fault that she was dead, but maybe I deserved . . . I don't know what, if anything, I deserve. She was sick for a while, but I didn't think too much of it. She had missed days of work, which she never did. She was a hard worker and never took time for herself. Then after so many missed days, her manager, some kind white man, came to the apartment to check on her. And he immediately took her to the hospital. Shouldn't someone in her family have done that? Someone should've checked on her and, seeing that she was so unwell, taken her to the hospital. But we weren't a people who went to the doctor very often. I was a kid, so I kinda had to have regular doctor visits, but I was always raised to be tough, to get back up and dust myself off, to not cry, to not admit when I was in pain. If anyone in the family saw that she was ill, the prevailing wisdom was that she would get better. Maybe I had told her to go to the hospital and she refused. Maybe I could've done more to save her. Maybe I didn't want to.

I felt guilty.

So many things are left unsaid in Black families, especially between parents and their queer children. I never got to come out to my mother. I think I would've sooner than later if I had the chance. I knew she had said she would never want a gay child when I was younger and within earshot, but I really feel she would've been fine with it eventually. Living in America had loosened the old girl up. All those pro-gay episodes of *The Golden Girls* we watched together must have seeped into her brain at some point. We had also started watching *Will and Grace* together, which premiered a year before she died. The woman loved her primetime sitcoms. As did her gay-ass son.

And despite our occasional animosity, I know she loved me and would never turn me out or reject me. Also, it's not like it would've come as *that* much of a surprise. I mean, the woman lived with me for fourteen years—either she saw it or just ignored it.

With my mother's and my shared love of TV comedy, it's fitting that I kind of got to come out to her vicariously through an episode of the Netflix series *Master of None*. Written by the show's co-creator Aziz Ansari and writer-producer Lena Waithe, "Thanksgiving" brought the Black coming-out experience into fresh, wonderful territory.

The episode follows Denise (Waithe) through a series of Thanksgivings with her mother, Catherine, played by Angela Bassett (and you know how I feel about Angela Bassett); her aunt (criminally underrated character actress Kym Whitley); her impossibly old grandmother (Venida Evans); and her best friend Dev (Ansari), whose Indian parents didn't celebrate the holiday.

Denise gradually comes out over these Thanksgivings, over the course of twenty-five years. The episode's first Thanksgiving is in 1992, then on Thanksgiving 1995 she begins to realize she has feelings for girls, eventually coming out to Dev on Thanksgiving 1999. They agree to use the term "Lebanese" as a matter of comfort for Denise. That always made me chuckle.

On one of the very gay episodes of *The Golden Girls*, 1986's "Isn't It Romantic?," Dorothy's (Bea Arthur) lesbian friend Jean (Lois Nettleton) comes to visit and falls in love with Rose (Betty White). When Dorothy tells Blanche (Rue McClanahan) that Jean is a lesbian, Blanche, thinking herself erudite and sophisticated, seems unfazed.

"You aren't surprised?" Dorothy's mother, Sophia (Estelle Getty), asks her.

"Of course not! I mean, I've never known any personally, but isn't Danny Thomas one?" She had confused "lesbian" for

"Lebanese," and soon she begins to turn the word over and over, finally realizing that Danny Thomas is, in fact, not one. "Lesbian . . . lesbian? . . . LESBIAN!" *Master of None*'s "Lebanese" bit felt like an homage to that other landmark lesbian episode of television.

Denise is hesitant to come out to her mother. Of course she would be. The predominant trope among Black mothers and their queer kids had been, at least until this episode, one of dismissal, disgust, and disownership. The alternative was simply not to talk about it. My mother and I just didn't talk about the pink elephant in the room, which was me lip-synching to Whitney Houston songs like my life actually did depend on it. It was my complete disinterest in girls or dating. It was my effeminacy, which didn't seem to go away as I got older, as others had predicted and hoped. We didn't talk about any of that; we just kept the peace while we could. There's peace in silence, but also enormous guilt.

Denise finally comes out to her mother at the most unusual of the Thanksgivings, one without the family and Dev, at a diner in 2006. Bassett is stunning in this scene. When Denise finally speaks her truth, her mother isn't upset that she's gay; she's upset that her life is going to be that much harder. "It is hard enough being a Black woman in this world," she tells Denise. "Now you want to add something else to that?"

For Catherine, being gay seems like a choice, but what people fail to understand is that most people, given the choice, wouldn't choose to make their lives harder. They wouldn't choose to be ostracized, to be vilified, criminalized, stoned, ridiculed.

Wearing a gorgeous pussycat wig, Bassett conveys so much complexity: she's disappointed, she's angry, she's partly relieved because the unsaid has finally been said, but above all, she's scared. Tearfully, Catherine tells Denise, "I just—I don't want life to be hard for you."

That scene always *guts* me. It's what I imagined, what I hoped, my mother would've said to me, could've said to me. My mother never told me she loved me. It just wasn't her style, effusive emotion. It would've been nice to have heard it, to truly know rather than to have to intuit her love. But I always wondered if she would've loved me if she had known all of me, if she would've accepted me, if she could've been like Catherine.

LUNETTE URLA BRATHWAITE was born on November 12, 1943, in Georgetown, Guyana. Her first name was Lunette, but she went by Urla instead. Back then, Guyana was still British Guiana, a colony under that empire on which the sun never set. It declared its independence on May 26, 1966. Urla was twenty-two. What did it feel like to wake up in a new country, or did it feel like nothing at all? Three years later she gave birth to my brother, Wayne.

When her younger sister, Una Patricia Brathwaite, my aunt Patsy, went to America, Urla did not. I don't know why. Maybe Patsy went for school or for work, and never looked back. She graduated, she married, she had kids, she got a job at IBM and a big house in Poughkeepsie, with a dog and an aboveground pool. What was Urla doing? Who was she? I would always ask her about her past in Guyana, but she never seemed to want to talk about it.

I, on the other hand, was fascinated. Unlike most of the kids I went to school with, I came from somewhere different and exotic, and that made me different and exotic. It was only natural I wanted to know more about it. I think she said she worked at a factory? How did she meet Carl Newton, my father? My father, who had other, full-grown kids. A handful of 'em. What were the circumstances? Do I even want to know? Of course I do. I'm nosy, and I love gossip.

Who was Urla Brathwaite? Was she lonely her whole life, like I've been? Did she crave love, only for it to be cruelly denied to her? Who was the man who knocked up a twenty-five-year-old woman in 1968 and didn't marry her? Did Urla not want to get married? Or was she left forever heartbroken? My mother will always remain a mystery to me, and thus a part of me will always remain unknowable.

Patsy filed for her older sister and her two sons to come to America, and we arrived in early January 1990. Wayne's birthday was later that month. He was turning twenty-one. I can understand how he could've gone wild as soon as he got here, confronted with this land of dreams and opportunity and women, so many women, so many white women, who were charmed by his good looks and accent. He just never grew older than twenty-one.

Wayne had two kids, a son named Wayne Jr. and a daughter, Jaiden, making me an uncle before I was eight. When we were on speaking terms, my brother and I barely spoke. We never had a real conversation. I guess he, too, will always remain a mystery to me, but that's a mystery I'm less interested in cracking. That we were never close made cutting him out of my life that much easier. But even those I'm close to are not immune to my cruelty. I've walked away from relationships before, including my friends, my brother, and the rest of my family, though I've had no lovers to abandon. And it's not as if I never think about the person again or don't regret the way things ended. But to my understanding, life is ephemeral, as are the bonds we make. Anyone can be taken from you at any moment. Love fades, friendships end, people die, and you keep moving.

MY AUNT MOVED fast, organizing a funeral for her sister in a matter of days. She died on Tuesday the second and was buried on the fifth of November, my birthday. My mother's was a week after mine. Scorpios. No wonder we were so often at odds. But Scorpios also love deeply, if not ostentatiously. I don't think my aunt realized what day she had chosen for the funeral, or maybe it wasn't much of a choice, maybe she just wanted to bury her sister as soon as possible and that was the soonest. And the most convenient. It was a Friday, after all.

But it was my fourteenth birthday, and for the rest of my life, my birthday will always remind me of the day my mother was buried. That, admittedly, messed me up a bit. For years it was a highly sensitive time, and I didn't know how to celebrate it. Or if I should celebrate it at all.

And it was just like two weeks of a shroud hanging over me, from the second when she died to my birthday/the anniversary of her funeral on the fifth, and then her birthday on the twelfth. I used to think it was a punishment, or a curse, that my living should always be directly tied to my mother's death.

That day exists in a fog of memory and yet . . . and yet . . . I can blink my eyes and be back there again because that day will always be a part of me. It is the clearest delineation between before and after. There was before that fifth of November and then there was everything after.

I'M FOURTEEN TODAY. Happy fucking birthday to me. I've waited for this day for so long, when I become a real teenager. Everyone knows thirteen doesn't count. At thirteen you're still a child. Today, I am a man. Or, at the very least, a teenage boy. I look over at my mom's bed. I'm still sleeping in the same room, still on my twin bed from Aaron's downstairs. It's more comfortable than that old hand-me-down box-spring nightmare, that's for sure. I want to sleep on my mom's bed because it's big and comfy and when she was at work I would always lay on it, though she told me not to, and I would rush to make the bed before she got home, in hopes she wouldn't notice. Now it's mine, I guess.

Wayne is still sleeping on the couch. But I can't sleep on it. How can I? She was just there two weeks ago. Covered in blankets. Barely moving. Barely breathing. My suit is hanging in the closet, right next to her clothes, which I also tried on when she wasn't home. She almost caught me in one of her dresses once. That heavily beaded, drop-waist burgundy number that zips up in the back. I always liked that dress on her. And it didn't look too shabby on me either. I was trying it on, you know, out of curiosity and boredom, when I heard her key in the lock. Shit! I panicked trying to get the dress off, but the zipper was stuck, so I shimmied out of it as quickly as I could and hung it back in place before she saw me. Then, in my first free moment, I smoothed out the dress and the zipper. I had zipped her up into that dress several times.

I hate that suit. It's too big. I'm too big. I look even fatter than I already am in it. On all the days I should look my cutest and thinnest, it's this. God, I can't wait for this day to be over. How am I going to get through it? You just get through it, Lester. You just get through it.

Wayne wishes me a happy birthday. I have to remember he also lost a mother. And they were together for a longer time; it was just them for like seventeen years before my big head came along. This can't be easy on him either. Be patient. Be patient. At least he remembered my birthday. Will anyone else? Probably not. How can I bring it up? I probably shouldn't bring it up, should I? Is that gauche? Is that what "gauche" means? I mean, it definitely feels inappropriate. "I'm sorry for your loss." "Thank you, but also, fun fact, it's my birthday." I should get money for this day. Lots of money. "It's your birth . . . oh, here's a twenty." Nah, that's definitely gauche. And gross. I guess I won't bring it up at all. Happy fucking birthday to me.

Hmm, wouldn't you know it? First time I get to ride in a

limo and it's for my mom's funeral. I can't even enjoy this glamour. I wonder if this is how Princes William and Harry felt? We're around the same age, aren't we? Their mother died two years ago. I remember that. We were in Wildwood—me, Mom, and Aunt Patsy. It was a nice vacation, but then we heard the news about Princess Diana. We didn't have any connection to her or anything. I mean, maybe Mom and Aunt Patsy felt a closer kinship to the royal family than I did, being former and forever citizens of British Guiana, but I was still sad. She seemed like a nice lady, and girl could dress. What a terrible way to die, and to lose your mother that young, and have the world watching you in pity.

I don't have the world watching me, thank god. But all these people. They're going to be looking at me. "That poor orphan bastard." *No one's going to call you an "orphan bastard."* But they might think it. Everyone's going to be pitying me. Not Wayne so much. He's a grown-ass man. I'm still a kid. Little do they know that I'm fourteen now. Little do they care. It's just sad. "That poor boy," they'll all say. Or maybe they won't know what to say at all. Maybe they'll just leave me alone. That would be *great*. I don't want to be here; I don't want to be doing this.

Everyone keeps asking me if I'm okay. Wayne, Aunt Patsy, Uncle Wilton, Gordon, Sherman, Randy. I barely talk to my cousins; they're all so much older than me. I guess they care. They loved my mom, I think. Didn't they? Didn't I? I haven't cried. I haven't shed a single tear all week. What's wrong with me? I don't want to cry. I feel like I could at any moment, I feel I could break down at any moment, and I don't want to, not in front of everyone. If I just look out the window of this decent midsize limousine, I won't cry. I'll get through this. I have to get through this.

Oh great, I have to sit in the front of the church, where everyone can see me. Where they can see me cry. No. Not today, Satan. Oh, there's Mione and Marsha. Wayne's baby mamas. They loved my mom. And she loved them, and the grandkids they gave her. Baby Jaiden doesn't know what's going on. Lucky. Little Wayne doesn't either. He keeps asking, "Where's Grandma?" Fuck. His little voice keeps asking, and it's breaking my heart. My eyes are stinging. No. No. No, no, no, don't you do it. I lower my head and keep it there during the entire service just to keep myself from crying. You'll get through this. You have to get through this.

That was a close call. We're almost there. We just have to put her in the ground. Why did they pick this cemetery? It's right across the street from the Holiday Inn Express. What, are they gonna bury her in her uniform and rubber gloves, too? It's nice seeing her co-workers, though. They're so nice and seem really sad. Her manager, the man who took her to the hospital, shakes my hand, offering his condolences, and tells me if I ever need anything, etc., etc. I never want to step foot in that hotel again. But I thank him, my eyes still directed downward. The nice Haitian man who owns the store across the street from the apartment. Damn, that big belly is really straining against that jacket. I'm glad he's here, too. He also shakes my hand, offers his condolences, and tells me if I ever need anything I shouldn't hesitate to come to the store. All I have to do is ask. I say thank you and wait for this endless procession of mourning to pass.

I didn't want to go up to her casket. To "say goodbye." I

couldn't do it. I couldn't bring myself to do it, and no one forced me to. I don't have to do anything today. Just get through it. Shit, now it's raining? What is this? Who's that woman? That's quite the wig. Is that a wig on top of a wig? Must be a friend of my aunt's. You know, I used to think that was my aunt's real hair. My world was shattered when I realized it was all wigs. It was all fake. Oh god . . . the woman's singing. What song is this? Some hymn. She sounds beautiful . . . my heart is racing, my throat's dry, I can feel the stinging in my eyes. No, not here. Please, not here. I'm pleading to a god in whom I don't believe.

There's no stopping the tears. They start running, and then it's too late. I'm sobbing, wailing as they lower my mother into the ground, as this woman's voice carries her spirit away from me, and the sounds of my cries inspire those of others because there's no sadder sound than a child crying out for his mother. Wayne holds me close to him. I feel small next to him. I look up at him. I'll never be six foot, I think, not like him. Behind his sunglasses I see that he's crying, too, and it just makes me cry harder. I cry for all the guilt I carry. I cry for all the times we fought over nothing. I cry for calling her a bitch and not always being patient or understanding. I cry because I'm still a fucking child. I cry because I'll never truly know my mother, and she'll never truly know me. I cry for all the pain I've stored up, too afraid to release it, too afraid what others might think, too afraid to appear weak or effeminate. I cry because I've lost my mother and I have so much life left to live. So much that she'll never see. I cry because it's my birthday and this will always be what I remember, every year.

IN MY SENIOR year of high school, when I was taking up the life-altering task of applying to colleges, I knew exactly what I would write for my personal essay. I mean, what else could I write? My mother's death hung over nearly my entire high school career, save the first two months of my freshman year. Still, I had persevered, not without a few stumbles along the way, because I was determined to get the fuck out of Pough-keepsie.

I had something (exactly) like a 4.3 GPA, a pretty good but not great SAT score (1275, out of 1600, a number that still haunts me for no real reason except my own nerdy obsessive-ness), and a full plate of extracurriculars. I was a poor Black kid with no parents but with a strong academic record and ambi-tion to spare—affirmative action was made for people like me. I knew the perfect essay would put me over the finish line.

I called it "Happy Birthday," recounting, as I've done here, the day of my mother's funeral. After penning the first draft, I sought out the help of my English teacher, Ms. Ricketts, a Ja-maican woman with glasses perpetually at the lower bridge of her nose and pencils stuck in the hive of maroon-colored dreads she piled high on top of her head. That particular maroon ran its way through Black women's hair for years in my youth—I remember when my mother had gotten that same shade and I thought it a bit young for her (as a baby gay I had very definite opinions about my mother's, and everyone else's, style), but it grew on me.

I loved Ms. Ricketts—she had spent months teaching us

Song of Solomon, to the detriment of the rest of our course load, which wasn't great for our year-end exams, but was ultimately enriching for me, at least, one of the very few Black kids in her Honors English class. Naturally, I asked her to take a look at my essay.

One day after school, I nervously dropped by her classroom with the essay in hand. I had expected to just leave it with her and come back the next day for her notes, but she asked me to stay while she read it. I hate watching people read my work. I inevitably end up stealing glances, looking for signs of their reaction—do they love it? Did they get that joke? Can they feel me watching them? I'd rather just get feedback at a later date, but apparently that wasn't an option.

When Ms. Ricketts finished reading it, she took off her glasses and looked at me sympathetically. "This was very hard for you, wasn't it?"

It was and it always is. My mother's death still felt all too fresh in my head and so my writing, usually so fluid and alive, was stilted, halting. Ms. Ricketts had picked up on that. So she volunteered her time to help me work on the essay a couple days after school, between my other obligations.

When we met, she would just encourage me to talk. I was usually very silent in class. And really, everywhere, except with my closest friends, who knew how boisterous I could be. Otherwise, I *preferred* to be quiet. It's what I was most familiar with, what made me comfortable.

I kept so much inside, and yet there was *so much* inside. I found that I could release it in its purest form only through my writing, as speaking was always a struggle. I would have ideas in my head but my lips and my teeth and my tongue and my jaw would rebel, and the words would come out garbled, stuttering, too fast, too low. Whomever I was speaking to would invariably ask me, "What was that?" so that I spoke with the intention of having to repeat myself, with the intention of being misunderstood or not heard at all. Silence was easier.

And then there was the way I was raised. Kids of West Indian parents are taught to speak only when spoken to, to never interrupt an adult conversation, to be seen and not heard, and all that toxic bullshit that led me to bury my feelings so as to bury myself, to be invisible so that I never felt seen to begin with. So not only did I feel physically unable to verbalize how I felt, I didn't think I could or that I should. And that weighed heavily on me. Ms. Ricketts, as a West Indian woman, perhaps understood that, and she tried to help me to unburden myself.

She told me something I've never forgotten, because I had never thought of myself that way: "You have the kind of voice that when you talk, people listen." That felt like a lot of power. Power I was not ready to accept, not that I would know what to do with it. "But you're afraid of your own voice," she told me. She was right. I didn't know if I even wanted people to listen to me. It's why I ate my words before they were fully out of my mouth, for fear of being exposed, of being vulnerable.

I silenced myself, diminished my presence, as so often minorities do out of fear or the instinct to survive. I shrunk myself safely in the back of Ms. Ricketts's class and even when I knew the right answer or had an insightful remark, I stayed silent. What if I was wrong? What if no one understood what I said and I had to repeat it and what if then I stuttered over my words, revealing a weakness? Would they laugh at me, think me less smart, less worthy? I couldn't risk it.

But now Ms. Ricketts finally wanted to hear me, really *hear* me. She asked me to project, to open my mouth and project as loud as I could.

I gave her a good "AAAAAAAH!"

She smiled widely and threw her arms open and said, "Louder!"

"AAAAAAAAAAHHHHH!!!"

"Louder!" her arms and smile wider. I felt as if she was next going to have me stand on a desk and address her as "Captain, My Captain." And I would've. I thrived on the attention I got from my teachers, especially Black women. It was the attention—and more important, the understanding—I couldn't get at home.

Ms. Ricketts wanted me to realize the power of my voice, the power of expressing myself and being unafraid of doing so. In turn, I could finally write truthfully about that day, that fifth of November. By breaking my silence I was able to release just a bit of the pain I had buried that day with my mother.

My college essay was, I think, until this book, the most important thing I had written. It helped set me on the path of the rest of my life. And it taught me the importance of not just owning my voice, but owning my story. I turned the worst day of my life into the key to my future.

10

RAGE

To be a Negro in this country and to be relatively conscious is to be in a state of rage almost, almost all of the time—and in one's work. And part of the rage is this: It isn't only what is happening to you. But it's what's happening all around you and all of the time in the face of the most extraordinary and criminal indifference, indifference of most white people in this country, and their ignorance.

—James Baldwin

SO THERE'S NOTHING I can do about my rage, is that what you're telling me, Jimmy Baldwin? It's a part of me because I am Black, I am living in America, and I am conscious of being Black and living in America, as he said in a 1961 conversation with Langston Hughes, Lorraine Hansberry, Emile Capouya, and Alfred Kazin.

But the people I see most often in a constant state of rage in this country are not Black and are debatably conscious. I know my rage comes from being thrust into a system where I'm subject to any number of historical and societal inequities that are deliberately in place to impede my success. I have rage against my oppression—but white people done stole that, too. Black people have been saying the system is rigged for generations, with proof being the state of their very lives, but now white people can cite minor inconveniences and blatant lies as reasons for their righteous indignation over the system. The same system that has been rigged *for* them. That their lives are unsatisfactory or disappointing is the result of the system also being rigged against anyone who isn't rich enough to buy their way out of it.

No, to live in America, period, is to be in a state of rage almost all of the time. Strife is the national pastime. But more than anything, American rage is fueled by the bloody, destiny-manifesting history of America—one can never downplay the importance of history to what is happening now. It's simply everywhere. To be an American, to live in America, is to be angry. To be an American, to live in America, and to be at any social disadvantage—whether it be race, gender identity, sexual orientation, immigration status, religion, or what have you—is to embody and inspire rage, as well as to experience it wholly while having it visited upon you constantly.

This rage is fueled by entitlement to, and often the subsequent denial of, the American Dream. It is fueled by the denial of reparations, both financial and spiritual, made for centuries of enslavement enforced upon Black people. It is fueled by the machinations of the rich and powerful to maintain their wealth and power by keeping the lower classes distracted from said machinations. It is fueled by ignorance, it is fueled by "fake news," it is fueled by the unrelenting clip at which news and media are produced and consumed.

Our politicians have become clowns and fascists and hypocrites, beholden, regardless of party affiliation, to money and not to their constituents. America has never really had much of a moral leg to stand on, going back to the exploitation of indigenous people and then hundreds of years of slavery, followed almost immediately by Jim Crow, the internment of Japanese Americans, not to mention the myriad atrocities committed abroad, and way too many other things to list here. But the moral rot at the core of this country is eating us all alive.

Making it worse is the white indifference and white ignorance Baldwin mentions. White liberals are often accused, by the more radical on the political spectrum, of being indifferent to the capitalist excess at the root of nearly every problem in America. Instead, they choose to focus on appearing, rather than actually being, altruistic, in favor of their own comfort. Meanwhile, white conservatives are often accused of being ignorant by anyone who's not a white conservative. White liberals have a dogged determination to be affirmed in their own thinking, no matter how wrongheaded or racist. Traditional media and social media only serve to amplify tensions that are already running high. And next thing you know you got a bunch of white folks storming the Capitol.

Because of course they did. White people can do anything with their rage. They don't fear consequences, not the way Black folk do. The minute I saw what was going down on January 6, I knew if those rioters had been Black, the streets of DC would be running red with blood. Black people know they can't win in a war against this country. But we don't want war. Most of us don't; some of us would love to drive a tank right through Mar-a-Lago. We mostly just want to be treated fairly. But America has a way of treating fairness as an undue burden. Reconstruction, the only real and substantive attempt to reckon with the impact of slavery in America, lasted a good five years before the whites got tired of conceding anything and the Blacklash began in earnest. Those salty white treasonous bastards called it the Redemption. The historical lack of any sense of irony among white people would be hilarious if it weren't so atrocious.

Black rage has to be confined, to oneself, to one's home, to one's community, whereas no one is safe from white rage. White rage mows down kids in school, old ladies in church, random folks in supermarkets. White rage kills Black people with impunity. And so Black rage is also a product of impotence in the splotchy, pockmarked face of white rage. Martin Luther King Jr.'s nonviolent approach in the civil rights movement might have been effective, to a degree, but not all Black people have been satisfied with passivity.

Black nationalist movements date back to the mid-nineteenth century with renaissance man Martin Delany. They reached their peak in the early twentieth with Jamaican-born activist Marcus Garvey and found powerful voices in Malcolm X, Stokely Carmichael, and Huey Newton during the midpoint of that century. But before the white clown show stormed the Capitol in 2021, Black Panthers demonstrated at the California state capitol in 1967, armed to the teeth. They were there protesting, get this, a gun control bill, but their show of force inspired then governor Ronald Reagan to sign that bill into law, backed by, of all people, the National Rifle Association. Literally the only thing that can inspire the NRA to back gun control laws is Black folks with rifles.

In response to the obvious camaraderie between white militias and police officers, a Black nationalist militia formed in 2017 called the Not Fucking Around Coalition, or NFAC. They mostly showed up and marched, peacefully, at protests for racial justice, while defending their right to bear arms, the hill America will happily die on. Of course, a group of well-trained, heavily armed Black people can't go unchallenged for long. Delany is all but forgotten to history, Garvey was deported, Malcolm X was assassinated, the FBI discredited Carmichael, and America just broke Huey Newton. In 2022, the NFAC's leader, John Jay Fitzgerald Johnson, aka Grand Master Jay (not of Furious Five fame), was sentenced to seven years in prison for allegedly brandishing his gun at federal task force officers at a protest. Reader, please know that while typing that last sentence, my right hand paused out of instinct to mime a lazy hand job.

It's surprising there haven't been more Black militias, honestly. Well, it *would be* surprising if the FBI weren't so good at its job. Of being racist. Not that I'm calling for a race war, but Black people have every right to be angry, to arm themselves, to storm the fucking Capitol, and not because some power-drunk asshole told them to. It's the daily indignities, the historical atrocities, the generational trauma, the economic theft, and the refusal to apologize for any of it. Apology in the form of reparations, something that should've happened decades ago, but an idea that keeps regaining traction every few years. But America—its greedy politicians, their implicitly and explicitly racist white constituents, and the small-thinking white liberals who can't conceive of a way of not being on the hook for said reparations—doesn't believe in handouts, even when that money is owed, with hundreds of years of interest.

This indifference to Black trauma—you say sorry when you fucked up; that's just the human thing to do—will always foster rage in Black Americans. That they've had to fight tooth and nail for every right they have is beyond insulting when the entire economy of this wealthiest nation in the history of the fucking world was built on the broken backs of their ancestors. Their ancestors were each promised forty acres and a mule, but they were given 160 years and counting of institutional discrimination. It's barbaric. The Black rage that erupted into the streets in the summer of 2020 was about more than George Floyd or Breonna Taylor or the countless Black people killed with impunity by police. It was a primal howl for finally! fairness, finally! acknowledgment, finally! reparations, finally! A reckoning.

And then, as always, there was the Blacklash. Trump was the Blacklash to Obama, January 6 was the Blacklash to the previous summer's Great Reckoning. Whiteness refuses to accept any form of comeuppance, and as a result it's dragging us down into a hell of its own making. White people are like Dorothy in *The Wizard of Oz*, just lost and high on amphetamines (RIP Judy), running around with a bunch of questionable friends trying to solve a problem they've had the answer to all along. It's like, you're the assholes voting these other assholes into office off your grievances, who then do nothing to address those grievances. They just offer more grievances to keep themselves in power. Fix your mistakes, whites! But first, you have to admit you made them in the first place.

The American Condition is one of perpetual rage, which is why the most dangerous creature on the planet is an angry white American man. His power, his privilege, his predilection toward violence. Why is he angry? I've given up caring because the source of his rage no longer concerns me. We're all angry now. Visibly, palpably, as if we've been given permission, where, for so many years, white men took the permission without ever asking for it. The angry white man has been a trope through wars and movements in which he was the center of the story. White male rage was righteous, whereas every other kind of rage was destructive, hysterical, primal.

Todd Phillips's 2019 film *Joker* is among the most prominent, and popular, "angry white man" films of the past decade. There have been fewer and fewer of these kinds of films because there are more people of color and women behind and in front of the camera and so white men aren't the only ones who get to be angry anymore. Which makes white men angry. *Joker* spoke to the anger of the post-Trump white man, whether he was a Trump supporter or not. As a gay man, I've always been far more interested in Catwoman, Michelle Pfeiffer's peerless performance in 1992's *Batman Returns*, putting nearly all subsequent superhero film acting to shame. But while Catwoman slinks in the shadows waiting for her own movie (and the 2004 schlock fest starring Halle Berry does not count . . . and I saw it in theaters), the Joker pops up again and again—just recently, three actors portrayed him on film, in big films, within a six-year period.

Heath Ledger's iconic performance in *The Dark Knight*—the only performance to come close to Pfeiffer's—spawned an army of imitators who menacingly asked, "Why so serious?" Jared Leto had big shoes to fill in 2016's *Suicide Squad*, and he did not fill them. Joaquin Phoenix, however, won a Best Actor Oscar for his acclaimed turn in Phillips's *Joker*. The film was an amalgamation of Martin Scorsese's *Taxi Driver* and *The King of Comedy*, both superior films, both starring Robert De Niro acting the shit out of the screen. Both are also about angry white men, with 1976's *Taxi Driver* perhaps being the ultimate example. 1982's *The King of Comedy* is a bit more mercurial, less why-so-serious.

In *Taxi Driver*, De Niro stars as Travis Bickle, a young, lonely, insanely hot (I'm sorry, '70s De Niro was . . . *it*) cabdriver who becomes more and more disconnected from society and takes it upon himself to rid New York's filthy streets of the "scum" that disgusts him. He's like Batman but poor. Which makes him a criminal. But also an antihero. Because he just wants to help, in his own way. And that way is intensely violent. On the other hand, De Niro's *King of Comedy* character, Rupert Pupkin, has no savior complex; he just wants to tell jokes. He, too, is a lonely, white, hot ('80s De Niro could still catch it) man, but his anger is less obvious. Still, his entitlement—to fame and fortune, the late-twentieth-century American Dream—is strong. Pupkin eventually resorts to kidnapping his idol,

Jerry Langford (Jerry Lewis), and forcing his way onto Langford's late-night talk show to do his routine.

Joker takes a similar premise: a would-be stand-up comedian obsessed with an older would-be mentor, Murray Franklin, played, in a meta move, by De Niro. But Phoenix's Arthur Fleck is more Travis Bickle than Rupert Pupkin, and De Niro gets his aging but still hot head blown to pieces in the final act. On live television. And audiences, mostly white men, fell in love with this character. *Joker* was a huge box office hit and was nominated for and won multiple awards, with Phoenix particularly, and rightfully, singled out for his performance.

Still, some felt that *Joker*, like all movies about angry white men who turn to violence, often on a massive scale, glamorized and sympathized with the murderous and mentally ill Fleck. His profile was too close for comfort to the angry white men who shoot up public spaces IRL. And of course it glamorized him. Sure, it's up to the audience whether they choose to sympathize with a character, but the filmmaker made the choice to paint Arthur Fleck cum the Joker as a victim. Another poor white man abandoned by society, whose mental illness went unchecked by a failing system. The profile of every mass shooter in America.

The Joker is not an antihero. He's just a straight-up irredeemable villain. And he's Batman's boyfriend or something, because the two of them have a serious hard-on for each other. The Joker is a psychopath, but he's dressed as a clown and does ridiculous, comical stunts that still kill people. Catwoman is an antihero because she had reasons, sometimes altruistic ones, for the bad things she does. Antiheroes seek justice, their own idea of justice, outside of traditional means. The Joker just seeks chaos. And people love chaos. Well, white men love chaos—because they're the only ones who benefit from it.

Chaos represents tearing it all down, burning it to the ground, destroying the order of things, and that always hurts the most vulnerable in society. White men, however, would remain (or at least assume they will remain) at the top of the social hierarchy amid this chaos, just as white men now reign over the chaos of modern-day America. The Joker is wish fulfillment, the ability to have it all come crashing down and making a quip about it at just the right moment. A dozen people were fatally shot at a Home Depot. Why so serious?

Movies like *Joker* fetishize violence just in the casualness with which someone gets their fucking head blown off. When people are shot in TV shows or movies or video games, it's just bang bang and you move on to the next. You don't see the victim struggling for life for minutes on the ground, lying in a pool of their own blood, their intestines collapsing out of their rapidly dying body before they shit themselves. And even if you do, it doesn't register because it's just a TV show or movie or video game. It's not real.

But when it is real, I can't bring myself to look. Movies can make a killing so visceral, so up close, and in such high definition—but blurry dashcam footage is a bridge too far. I can't watch Black people being hurt or killed in real life, not only out of sensitivity to it, but because of the sensitivity of it. I don't want to watch it so often that it loses meaning, like violence has in every other corner of our society. Though sometimes I think it might behoove the public to release footage of mass shootings just so people can see what it means, so that it's not just a flurry of headlines and numbers and places: Six Dead in Gainsborough, Eight Slain in Anaheim, Thirteen Slaughtered in Burlington. But they happen so often, what's to keep us from getting inured to this damning footage just as easily?

THE ANGRY WHITE man has given way to the angry other. Rage is no longer the sole domain and privilege of white men. In the 2023 Prime Video series *Swarm*, co-created by multi-hyphenate Donald Glover, Dominique Fishback stars as Dre, an obsessed fan of a Beyoncé-like superstar who kills offenders who have slighted her queen online. Serial killers are overwhelmingly white men, and television about white male serial killers has frequently been criticized for, again, sympathizing with brutal murderers. But I liked sympathizing with Dre.

I'm not a card-carrying member of the Beyhive, but I'm like a two-step away from that level of standom. Standom devotion is blind and unquestioning, like religion, and I've never been a fan of religion. But as a gay, I ride hard for my divas and don't take kindly to anyone talking shit about them. Would I murder for Janet or Whitney or Bey? Probably not. We'll see where life takes me, but. Probably. Not. Beyond her motives, I sympathized with Dre because she was Black, a Black woman on top of that. Black women are usually the victims in most murderous narratives—Zazie Beetz was the object of Joaquin Phoenix's deranged attention in *Joker*, though she avoids a grisly end—and there Dre was killing folks with impunity like a white man. Equality, y'all!

Glover and his *Swarm* co-creator Janine Nabers had seen years of blameless white so-called antiheroes on television— Tony Soprano, Don Draper, Walter White—and they wanted to create a character in that similar archetype but as a Black woman. Dre is an antihero because she has a reason for her murders and we get to know her before she becomes a killer. So much of being an antihero is having a backstory. Once they're a fully fledged character, it's hard to condemn their actions outright. Dre is guilty over the death of her foster sister, who also loved their idol Ni'Jah, *Swarm*'s Beyoncé surrogate, and killing Ni'Jah's detractors is her way of preserving her sister's memory. Both Nabers and Fishback insist *Swarm* is a show, ultimately, about sisterhood. But it comes in bloody packaging, which is brilliant.

In a television landscape overcrowded with too much damn content, not nearly enough of it any good, *Swarm* broke through in a way most shows cannot because it understood the landscape into which it was entering. Stunts were pulled. The show had Malia Obama in the writers' room; guest stars like Paris Jackson and Billie Eilish, the latter in her acting debut; and enough Beyoncé parallels to prompt a lawsuit. But above all, Dre was unlike any character seen on television. An angry Black woman who got away with it. She isn't punished for her rage; if anything, she's rewarded for it, which is something that never happens in America.

I chose to sympathize with Dre because as a Black person in America, I understand the urge to want to kill, and so for me, she was my wish fulfillment. White boys get Soprano, and Draper, and White, and Joker, and Joker, and Joker, as surrogates for their rage, and with *Swarm* I got mine. What does it say that we all apparently want to murder one another, though?

AFTER HIS WHOLE "in a state of rage almost, almost all of the time" observation, Baldwin went on to say something that hit particularly close to home: "To be a Negro writer," he began, "at some point you have to decide that you can't spend the rest of your life cursing out everybody that gets in your way." To be a writer, he continued, you have to decide that "the suffering of any person" is "universal." Even though I am in a constant rage, I've developed an empathy as a writer that keeps me from being fully consumed by that rage. I can understand why a rich white man might be angry—change, fear, guilt—but that doesn't mean I have to agree with him. People, when you deal with them one on one, are mostly reasonable. It's when you get them in a group, and get 'em all worked up, that nuance flies out the door. Is thrown out of the door, really. *Fresh Prince* style.

I know I've had challenges as a poor Black queer immigrant, that my life has been harder than most, but I think when you've suffered a lot, you tend to have more empathy for the suffering of others. That's part of the reason why Black people have had a wealth of patience for white people. The Black church and its promise of glory in the afterlife is the other part. White man's religion has kept Black people docile since the days of slavery, while also providing a respite from the turmoil and tragedy of their lives inflicted by white men. The white man, then, is both savior and persecutor, god and devil. But he is only human and vulnerable to lies, to fear, to ignorance. I can hope that even the worst among them can be changed when shown the error of their ways. As I'm not religious, however, I only *hope* for the best in people. I don't blindly believe in it.

This hope, however, is what prevents me from cursing out everybody who gets in my way. Not just hope for the best in people, but hope for the best in myself. I stopped cursing people out (and I really used to do so . . . a lot) because I hated the way it made me feel. Any sense of victory or accomplishment is almost immediately replaced by guilt. It doesn't feel good to hurt someone else's feelings. Not when I'm fully aware that this person might be having a shit day, that this might not be the best version of themselves, that they're probably experiencing their own pain. As a moody bitch, I know I'm not always my best self and that a warm smile and friendly greeting can go a long way. I can go into a situation expecting the worst, just ready to fight, but disarm me with kindness and I'm as harmless as a kitten. Sometimes all we really need is for someone to be nice to us.

Simply put, when I realized the world didn't revolve around me, to my great chagrin, I also realized that not everyone is feeling what I'm feeling or knows what I'm feeling. Therefore, I can't blame them for that. I can't blame them for not knowing my innermost thoughts. And as a writer my mind tends to wander, so that I observe people and wonder what they're going through, what they're thinking. I accept the fact that others have an interior life to which I am also not privy. And who am I to assume anything about them?

Now don't get me wrong: When I'm on my Michelle Obama kick and go high when they go low, sometimes I still wish I *had* cursed someone the fuck out. But ultimately I'm glad I didn't. What if I see them again? Then we're permanent enemies based on one unfortunate, and probably so fucking stupid, interaction.

In all stoned seriousness, the world would be a much chiller place if everyone just smoked weed. I started when I was around eighteen and that in turn started the very long process of my calming the fuck down. I'm high all the time. At this point, it's a public service. Not-high me would for sure be cursing everybody out, throwing hands and shade out in these streets. Weed not only helps me keep calm and makes me less anxious, but it also helps with my writing. My flights of fancy are operated by Blunt Airlines on the Bong 7420. Is being stoned a crutch? Of course it is. So is religion, but who doesn't need a crutch in life? This bitch'll kick the legs right from under you.

If only weed could replace guns as America's favorite vice. You want guns off the street? Set up a weed-for-guns buyback program. For every gun someone turns in, they get an ounce of weed—maybe a pound for automatic rifles, as added incentive. Mass shootings would drop, vibes would increase exponentially, and think of all the tax dollars from federally legalizing weed. That could pay for, like, a universal basic income or some shit. But then again, I'm high and I am also giving the US government far too much credit. UBI? In this economy?

. . . Yeah, come to think of it, that'd actually be pretty awesome.

Even though I'm stoned all the time, my rage hasn't disappeared. It's still there, resting under billowing clouds of blunt smoke, dormant but easily stirred. My rage has become something like a low, discordant chord always humming in the back of my head, threatening to crescendo at the most inopportune moments. The weed and my rage intermingle in the strangest ways, so at times I'm just pissed and high, quietly fuming and getting the munchies. I really don't think there's any getting rid of my rage, just managing it or, as Baldwin wrote in 1955's *Notes of a Native Son*, learning "to live with it, consciously." But as an artist, I have another option, something Black artists have been doing for decades, centuries, and that's to *channel* my rage.

Baldwin's good buddy Nina Simone wrote "Mississippi Goddam," which she christened her first civil rights song, in under an hour. She later recalled that the song "erupted out of me quicker than I could write it down." She wrote it in response to the killing of four Black girls in the 1963 bombing attack of the 16th Street Baptist Church in Birmingham, Alabama. "At first I tried to make myself a gun. I gathered some materials. I was going to take one of them out, and I didn't care who it was," Simone said after hearing of the Birmingham bombing. "Then Andy, my husband at the time, said to me, 'Nina, you can't kill anyone. You are a musician. Do what you do.' When I sat down the whole song happened. I never stopped writing until the thing was finished."

Having heard Simone recall the time she pulled out a gun and shot at a record company executive while demanding her money (she missed, but she was "sorry I didn't get him"), I'm sure that Ms. Simone wasn't kidding about taking "one of them out." That act might've been cathartic, but it would've only served to end her life, or at least end her freedom. But "Mississippi Goddam," which was also inspired by the murders of Emmett Till and Medgar Evers, both in Mississippi, had a much larger impact than what one act of violence in response to another could possibly hope to achieve.

The song didn't end racism; it didn't make sense out of the senseless deaths of those little girls or that little boy or that young man. But it expressed a shared outrage. It highlighted injustice. She performed and recorded it in 1964 at Carnegie Hall in front of an audience of mostly white people who didn't know what to make of it. Some folks, particularly in the South, protested the song. "We got several letters where they had actually broken up this recording and sent it back to the recording company, really, telling them it was in bad taste," Simone said in a 1964 interview on *The Steve Allen Show.* "They missed the whole point."

They sure did, Nina. The outrage was at the song, not at the events that had inspired it. So often, particularly amid our social media frenzy, people get caught up in how something is said rather than what is being said. Because it's easier that way, and, more important, it avoids having real and necessary conversations. Writing and performing "Mississippi Goddam" may have been a way for Nina Simone to channel her rage, but it didn't lead her to finding any peace. She wrote in her autobiography about how lonely she felt being part of the civil rights movement, just like she "had been lonely everywhere else."

Her whole life, she sometimes thought, had "been a search to find the one place I truly belong." That sounds familiar. She felt betrayed by America and the stagnant pace of change. She would eventually abandon America, her husband, and her child, and she fell out with her father and refused to visit him on his deathbed. Plagued by a ceaseless rage—and, it must be said, mental illness; she had bipolar disorder—Simone alienated fans and friends alike, but her rage is her greatest legacy.

Sure, every car commercial, TikTok, and karaoke night has taken the joy out of "Feeling Good" and the charm out of "I Put a Spell on You," but Nina Simone continues to inspire because of the fervor of her genius and how she used it to spark a light in the dark. "She never stopped speaking out against injustice," Simone's daughter, Lisa, told her biographer Alan Light (via a 2022 *Vanity Fair* article). "I think that Mom's anger is what sustained her, really what kept her going. It just became who she was."

That also sounds familiar . . . sorta like a low, discordant chord humming in the back of my head. Rage can, of course, be destructive. But whenever I've felt as if I had nothing, I knew I always had my rage, my rage at being denied what I thought was owed to me and the rage exacerbated by my persistent loneliness and poverty. I would channel that rage into my writing or into my workouts; it would fuel my drive to be better, it would ignite my will to survive, not just survive but to thrive!

So then I might have a certain reluctance to fully let go of my rage even if I could, for fear that if I didn't have that old reliable hum in the back of my head, I wouldn't have anything when times inevitably got hard. Rage is a fire. It's not just uncontrollable anger, but a manifestation of passion. It's forever a part of me, not just because I'm Black but because I am alive and I have an unrelenting passion for this life. I know what was sacrificed so that I might be here today, and I don't take that sacrifice lightly. I have to live for my mother, as either penance or benediction.

It's not that I love being alive or that I'm in love with the world and all its wonders! Being alive sucks a lot of the time. "I hate it here" has been a favorite mantra of mine for the past few years especially. But I consider this life a gift, and being alive a miracle; that you or I should exist at all in this cold, vast universe is extraordinary. In all that vastness, my rage is beyond insignificant, but that very rage is my lifeblood. In a way, rage is the lifeblood of the universe. Rage is atoms exploding and molecules crashing into one another; it's the hearth fires and holocausts banked down inside of stars and inside of me.

To simply be alive is to be in a state of rage all the time! The world rages around you, always, just as thoughts and ideas, wants and desires, rage inside of you. Always. Rage, then, doesn't always need to be uncontrollable or destructive; it can be propulsive, restorative. Revolutions are born of rage. Change is forced through rage. Progress can be made through rage. But that requires a focused, controlled rage. When rage is unfocused, or focused on the wrong thing, that's just a precursor to chaos.

WHEN BALDWIN MADE his comments about being in a rage almost all the time, in 1961, the racial climate was slightly worse than it is now. Okay, it was much worse. I can admit that sixty-plus years have made some difference in the way Black people are treated in this country, but it's still only sixty years. That's a very short amount of time to completely upend the social order. Too short. That "we've come a long way, but there's a long way to go" isn't surprising, when you put sixty years in the context of four hundred years.

Despite having the style, disposition, and bedtime of an eighty-year-old widow, I was not, in fact, alive sixty years ago. But I know for a fact that it's better now being a Black man than it was back then. Truly, I'm living in the best time in American history to be a queer Black man. I can be gay. Openly. Out in these streets. Tits out, cheeks flapping. I can, in theory, get married, but in reality—good luck, sis. I can kiss a white boy in public and not get stoned to death or lynched. Well, at least not in New York. I mean, that *is* a comforting thought . . . I guess.

I have an illusion of freedom my forefags couldn't even dream of. But it's still an illusion, because the apparatuses that oppressed those who came before me are still very much intact—white supremacy, patriarchy, capitalism. Not until those systems are dismantled can any of us truly be free. I'm not saying to "tear it all down." Just tear down the really terrible parts that are, you know, killing the planet. Nor am I saying I know how to go about making *any* of that change. Like, if I did, throw a Nobel Peace Prize in my face. But the first step in destroying an enemy is identifying it. As minorities gain more power, the threat of the destruction of those systems grows and becomes more and more a reality. And that terrifies white people, particularly those desperately clinging to power. I fear they would rather see America implode than relinquish their death grip on this country.

And that's where rage comes in handy.

What I've learned is my rage isn't just unfiltered anger, but rather a logical reaction to having seen too much of the world too soon. To be young, gifted, Black, queer, and containing multitudes is to know your place in the world before you're able to fully understand the why of it all. Despite this knowledge, I love America, even though it seems to abhor me from time to time. I know my love might not seem evident since I criticize this country as constantly and harshly as a stereotypical Jewish mother, but like a Jewish mother, I do it out of love.

I loved learning about American history, the way all these people worked together for a common idea and changed the course of the world. I loved the fantasy of America I was sold by *Schoolhouse Rock*, "The Great American Melting Pot," a country made great by our differences, that welcomed everyone to its shores. I guess that was a popular fantasy all around the world. But that's all it was. Fantasy. America is still the land of opportunity; it's just that opportunity is scarce and not everyone is "deserving" of it.

Yet look at me. Take a good long stare, I don't mind. I came to this country when I was four, lost my only parent ten years later, went through any number of hardships and setbacks, and now you're reading my book. That's America, folks. It's also luck, and talent, and tenacity, and any number of other factors, but I couldn't be leading this life I lead back in Guyana. Or in many other places on this planet. I remember joking with my friends during Michelle Obama's 2016 Democratic National Convention speech, about the part when she says, "America is the greatest nation on earth." We were like, *Is it, though?* Maybe at the *exact moment* when she was speaking that was true, but at any other time, maybe top ten. And that's a big maybe. But greatest? America doesn't have the range for that.

I wonder about other places, though. Now more than ever I feel the need to get out of America. All signs point to "Fall of the Roman Empire." I don't know if that means leaving permanently, but I want to be somewhere else for a while. While I still can. Maybe Michelle Obama was right—she usually is—and America is the greatest nation on earth, but I'd like to see that for myself. I'd like to see other ways of living, perhaps find a country that more aligns with my values and finally quenches my dire thirst for love. The Black expat has always carried a romanticism for me: Josephine Baker, Nina Simone, James Baldwin. They, and so many other Black and queer American artists, found that they had to leave the confines of their own country in order to truly be free.

Free from the burden of expectation America places on you, on your work, on your body. Free from the stress of existing on land that broke the bones of one's ancestors. Free to define who you are, free to find who you might be and have been all along. This freedom, too, is an illusion because of course Black folks are discriminated against on multiple continents and in multiple languages. But the whole world can't be awful. Can it? . . . No! . . . Well, let's hope not.

I guess I'm struggling with my faith in America, in the world. In the broadest, most general terms. As if America is one thing, as if the world could be easily reduced to a single idea. I struggle sometimes with defining what it is I'm mad at because it feels like everything is terrible. I'm mad at injustice in all its forms, and I'm mad at Americans' increasing indifference to the truth, and I'm mad at indifference toward climate change. I'm mad at war, at microaggressions, at macroaggressions. I'm mad at white men for existing, mad at white men for not wanting me, at white women for being complicit. I'm mad at Black people for not rising up and taking what is ours, I'm mad at myself for not doing more, for not caring more, for not wanting to be better. I'm mad because I can't get the boy I want, or the recognition I want, or the body I want. I'm mad because this rage is all I've ever known and because I know that if I wanted to, I could scream as easily as taking a breath. I'm mad because I don't know what else to feel when everything feels too much and not enough. I'm mad that I have also grown numb to the way things are and will always be and there's nothing I can do about it. It's all so big and so much to consider and so overwhelming.

But I don't have to face these issues all alone. I couldn't if I wanted to. And none of us should have to face the problems of the world alone because we all live in the world, together. It is in the best interest of everyone to see that this ship doesn't sink. We have to shake ourselves free of apathy and despair and get mad at the assholes keeping us from a healthy planet, from robust education, from healthcare, from a living wage, from universal housing, from a world free of poverty and hunger, from basic needs and wants that we can almost all agree on but are led to believe are impossible. Collective rage is our only chance for survival.

In 2008, diva shaman Erykah Badu came out with her third studio album, *New Amerykah, Part One: 4th World War*, a rumination on the American Dream's failures for Black people. On the seventh track, "Twinkle," Badu modernizes Peter Finch's prescient monologue as mad-as-hell anchor Howard Beale from 1976's *Network*: "I want you to get mad!" Beale originally says. "I don't want you to protest. I don't want you to riot. I don't want you to write to your congressman because I wouldn't know what to tell you to write. I don't know what to do about the depression and the inflation and the Russians and the crime in the street. All I know is that first, you've got to get mad. You've gotta say, 'I'm a human being, goddammit! My life has value!'" Badu's version repeats Beale's speech nearly word for word because it remains far too prescient, even nearly fifty years later.

To be angry is to be aware. On the following track, "Master Teacher," Badu coined the term "woke," as in "I stay woke." Rage effectively leads to an a-wokening. "Woke" has since been co-opted by ruddy-faced racists turned fascists—congresspeople, governors, former presidents—as the symbol of everything they're fighting against, which is true: they detest, they fear enlightenment. Those ruddy-faced racists want to keep their followers ignorant and dim to maintain their own power. They want you to be angry, too, but at one another, not at them. They want us to be mad at superficial differences, at stupid things that don't matter, rather than at the deep institutional flaws they ignore to our great detriment.

Politicians know the power of rage. They are imperfect vessels for change, but they should not be mistaken as the agents of change. They are merely people charged with doing a job, and if they suck at it, they shouldn't be doing it. But the job is to serve the will of the people, not to serve their own whims. And the people have very basic needs—food, shelter, health-care, and education that's actually affordable and maybe a planet that's not trying to actively get rid of us because we're killing it—that are not being met. So what are we doing about it? While it's imperative that we hold our elected officials accountable, moreover, we have to resist the stubborn human desire for a savior.

No one person can save us. No one person has the answers. We have to give enough of a damn to save our fucking selves. We can't ignore our rage or succumb to it, but we must live with it consciously. We have to get mad as hell and refuse to take it anymore, as Howard Beale instructed all those decades ago. The only thing is, rage without direction or purpose just creates more chaos. Focused rage, though—that's some scary shit. Focused rage can topple institutions, demolish ideologies, rally revolutions, step on the gas of progress, or simply destroy us all. In order to survive on this planet together, we have to believe we're in this together and channel the ever-present rage and anxiety and angst of living in this world in this time into the only thing that matters today: the promise of tomorrow. Without which there's no will to change, no hope for anything better . . . there's . . . nothing.

So in the words of every rapper faced with the ubiquitous specter of haters: Stay mad. It might be the only thing that saves us.

ACKNOWLEDGMENTS

Gurl. This book took a lot out of me, and so I have a lot of people to thank for just keeping me alive and schticking. Thanks, first, to my second mom, Lauren. To my forever sister Krista. To my friend-family Gigi, Jenn, Paris, Jessica, and the kids from the bleachers at PHS; to my ride-or-dies Andres, Alby, and Cat; to my main gays Leon, Dane, Caleb, Julian, Brandon, Jeff, Liz, even Paul (thanks for the advice early on); to Marcos and his parents, Eloise and Larry; special shout-out to Ben and Chris for housing me in one of my many times of need; to Alec and Brooks and their house in Ptown, where I've escaped to write and/or catch my breath; to Jon and Bridgit; to Kelly, who offered me a place to stay in Ptown literally hours after we met; to Debby and Miguel for making LA bearable; to my sister Mac; to my brother and daddi Zac; to Gurlshine; to Leigh and Raisler; to Peter; to the *FashionIndie/Lookbooks* crew— including Ryan, Brad, Sam, Manny, and Jenn—for taking a chance on me and giving me my first writing job; to the *Out* crew—including Aaron, Jason, Matt, and Greg—for making my teenage dream come true with a place on the masthead of *the* formative magazine of my gay youth; to my wonderful teachers over the years, including, but not limited to, Ms. Howard, Mrs. DiMaso, Ms. Ricketts, Mr. Zinsley, Mr. Daniels, Mrs. Nichols, and Ms. Glozier; to Ms. Kenney and Isis; to my nephew, Wayne; to my editor Emi; to Amber, who helped me shape this book in the early stages; to Phoebe and the entire Tiny Rep fam for believing in me and this book; to my agent Robert for asking the question I'd been waiting for my entire life: "Do you have a book in you?"; to Diana Ross, just 'cause; to anyone I've forgotten who's helped me, acknowledged me, made me feel seen, or loved. Just . . . fucking thanks.

NOTES

―

CHAPTER 2: I WORSHIP AT THE ALTAR OF HIS BODY

43 **Black men are already perceived:** John Paul Wilson, Kurt Hugenberg, and Nicholas O. Rule, "Racial Bias in Judgments of Physical Size and Formidability: From Size to Threat," *Journal of Personality and Social Psychology* 113, no. 1 (March 2017): 59–80, https://www.apa.org/pubs/journals/releases/psp-pspi0000092.pdf.

45 **Only in 2022:** Jenn Abelson, Nate Jones, and Ladka Bauerova, "Built and Broken: Bodybuilders Dying as Coaches and Judges Encourage Extreme Measures," *The Washington Post*, December 7, 2022, https://www.washingtonpost.com/investigations/interactive/2022/bodybuilding-extreme-training.

49 **steroid use has been linked:** Kurt Skårberg, Fred Nyberg, and Ingemar Engström, "The Development of Multiple Drug Use Among Anabolic-Androgenic Steroid Users: Six Subjective Case

Reports," *Substance Abuse Treatment, Prevention, and Policy* 3 (November 2008): 24, https://substanceabusepolicy.biomedcentral.com/articles/10.1186/1747-597X-3-24.

51 **Hell, AIDS patients:** Thomas Zambito, "Serostim (HGH) on Black Market for Body Builders," New York *Daily News*, June 2, 2003, https://www.natap.org/2003/june/060903_8.htm.

CHAPTER 4: MEMOIR OF A BLOUSE

91 **When Trump told:** Jason Lemon, "Trump Tells Gay Supporter 'You Don't Look Gay' at Mar-a-Lago Fundraiser," *Newsweek*, March 31, 2022, https://www.newsweek.com/trump-tells-gay-supporter-you-dont-look-gay-maralago-fundraiser-1693931.

94 **Daniels told *Ebony*:** #TeamEBONY, "Lee Daniels: 'I Am Not Tyler Perry,'" *Ebony*, February 27, 2014, https://www.ebony.com/lee-daniels-i-am-not-tyler-perry-981.

97 **The producer of the track:** Jason Newman, "Flashback: The Notorious B.I.G. Rhymes as Lil' Kim in 'Queen Bitch' Demo," *Rolling Stone*, May 26, 2020, https://www.rollingstone.com/music/music-news/biggie-smalls-lil-kim-queen-bitch-demo-1003929.

CHAPTER 7: VICTIM OR VILLAIN?

162 **Smollett's family released:** Lester Fabian Brathwaite, "Smollett Family Responds to Attack: 'Jussie Is a Warrior Whose Light Cannot Be Dimmed,'" Logo News, January 31, 2019, https://www.logotv.com/news/4kmfaq/smollett-family-statement-jussie-smollett.

163   **The next day:** Lester Fabian Brathwaite, "The Audacity to Be Young, Black, and Gay," Logo News, January 30, 2019, https:// www.logotv.com/news/pkugg0/the-audacity-to-be-young-black -and-gay.

166   **"The most important thing that I can say":** Dominic Patten, "Jussie Smollett Defiant Against 'MotherF***ers' Attackers in 1st Public Appearance Since Alleged Assault," *Deadline*, February 2, 2019, https://deadline.com/2019/02/jussie-smollett-assualt-first -appearance-troubadour-lee-daniels-maxine-waters-weho -1202548463.

166   **"During times of trauma":** Cori Murray, "Jussie Smollett Breaks His Silence After Vicious Attack: 'I'm OK,'" *Essence*, February 1, 2019, https://www.essence.com/entertainment/only -essence/jussie-smollett-breaks-silence-vicious-attack.

166   **Two weeks later:** Dakin Andone and Ryan Young, "Two Arrested in Connection to the Attack on 'Empire' Star Jussie Smollett Are Released Without Charge," CNN Wires, February 16, 2019, https://fox2now.com/news/two-arrested-in-connection-with -attack-on-empire-star-jussie-smollett-are-released-without -charge/.

175   **"The great replacement is very simple":** Thomas Chatterton Williams, "The French Origins of 'You Will Not Replace Us,'" *The New Yorker*, November 27, 2017, https://www.newyorker.com /magazine/2017/12/04/the-french-origins-of-you-will-not -replace-us.

176 **When reached by** *The Washington Post*: Joe Heim and James McAuley, "New Zealand Attacks Offer the Latest Evidence of a Web of Supremacist Extremism," *The Washington Post*, March 15, 2019, https://www.washingtonpost.com/world/europe/new -zealand-suspect-inspired-by-far-right-french-intellectual-who -feared-nonwhite-immigration/2019/03/15/8c39fba4-6201 -4a8d-99c6-aa42db53d6d3_story.html.

180 **Within a series of emails:** Joseph Bernstein, "Alt-White: How the Breitbart Machine Laundered Racist Hate," BuzzFeed News, October 5, 2017, https://www.buzzfeednews.com/article/josephber nstein/heres-how-breitbart-and-milo-smuggled-white -nationalism.

CHAPTER 8: GIFTED

210 the **"most perfect feminine body"**: Schomburg Center for Research in Black Culture, Manuscripts, Archives and Rare Books Division, The New York Public Library. *The Hamilton Lodge Ball* (1939). Retrieved from https://digitalcollections.nypl.org/items /16acce70-7cf4-0133-d749-00505686d14e.

CHAPTER 10: RAGE

241 **as he said in a 1961 conversation:** thepostarchive, "'The Negro in American Culture' a Group Discussion (Baldwin, Hughes, Hansberry, Capouya, Kazin)," YouTube video, 1:37:02, https://www .youtube.com/watch?v=jNpitdJSXWY.

256 **"At first I tried":** Liz Fields, "The Story Behind Nina Simone's Protest Song, 'Mississippi Goddam,'" PBS.org, January 14, 2021,

https://www.pbs.org/wnet/americanmasters/the-story-behind -nina-simones-protest-song-mississippi-goddam/16651.

256 **Having heard Simone:** BBC HARDtalk, "Nina Simone on BBC HARDtalk, 1999," YouTube video, 24:25, https://www.youtube .com/watch?v=8olEruTT_io.

257 **She wrote in her autobiography:** Hadley Hall Meares, "The Burden of Brilliance: Nina Simone's Tortured Talent," *Vanity Fair*, April 6, 2022, https://www.vanityfair.com/hollywood/2022/04 /nina-simone-biography-old-hollywood-book-club.

ABOUT THE AUTHOR

LESTER FABIAN BRATHWAITE is a staff writer at *Entertainment Weekly* and, for some masochistic reason known only to him and his therapist, has been a professional writer for almost fifteen years. He has contributed to *The New Yorker, Rolling Stone*, and *The Advocate*, among other publications, and has also served as senior editor for *Out. Rage* is his first book.